21ST CENTURY SCIENCE

AIDS

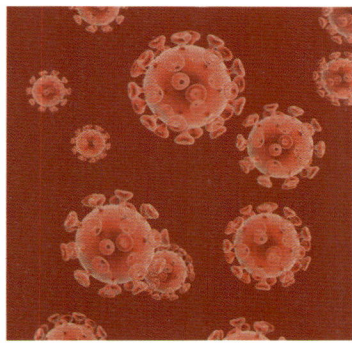
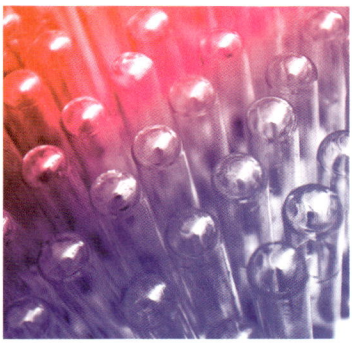

By Dr Susan Aldridge

ISBN: 978 1 84898 108 9 pbk

Copyright © TickTock Entertainment Ltd 2011
First published in Great Britain in 2011 by TickTock,
The Pantiles Chambers, 85 High Street, Tunbridge Wells,
Kent, TN1 1XP

Printed in China
3 5 7 9 10 8 6 4 2

The author has asserted her right to be identified as the author of this
book in accordance with the Copyright, Design and Patents Act, 1988.
The author and publisher would like to thank the following people for their help with describing
their work: Annabel Kanabus; Avert; Alex Cochrane; Institute of Biomedical Sciences.

Picture credits (t=top; b=bottom; c=centre; r=right; l=left; OFC= outside front cover;
OBC=outside back cover):

Courtesy of UNAIDS: 18–19. AFP/Getty Images: 22–23, 29, 30–31. Mark Baynes/Alamy: 57. Chris
Bjornberg/Science Photo Library: 8. Borderlands/Alamy: 52–53, 60–61.
Michael Brennan/Corbis: 33. BSIP, Beranger/Science Photo Library: 48. A. Dowsett,
Health Protection Agency/Science Photo Library: 6t. Eye of Science/Science Photo Library: 9.
Chris Gallagher/Science Photo Library: 49. Getty Images: 27, 55. Georg Hochmuth/epa/Corbis:
40–41. ISM/Science Photo Library: 15. iStock: OFC, 1ct (and throughout), 1cb (and throughout), 3H
(and throughout), 3I (and throughout), 34t. James King-Homes/Science Photo Library: 45.
Laguna Design/Science Photo Library: 16–17b. Will & Deni McIntyre/Science Photo Library: 20, 47.
Hank Morgan/Science Photo Library: 21. National Cancer Institute/Science Photo Library: 50–51.
NIBSC/Science Photo Library: 4–5, 58. Jim Olive, Peter Arnold Inc./Science Photo Library: 59.
David Parker/Science Photo Library: 44. Feije Riemersma/Alamy: 55. Shutterstock: 1tl (and
throughout), 1bl (and throughout), 1tr (and throughout), 1br (and throughout), 2l (and throughout),
6–7, 11l, 13t, 24t, 25, 35, 36–37, 38, 39, 42–43 (all). Paul Sutherland/Getty Images: 12t. Peter
Treanor/Alamy: 56. Robert Harding Picture Library/SuperStock: 26. TEK Image/Science Photo
Library: 16t. Keith Weller/US Department of Agriculture/Science Photo Library: 10 (main).

Every effort has been made to trace copyright holders, and we apologize
in advance for any omissions. We would be pleased to insert the appropriate
acknowledgements in any subsequent edition of this publication.

NOTE TO READERS
The website addresses are correct at the time of publishing. However, due to the ever-changing
nature of the Internet, websites and content may change. Some websites can contain links
that are unsuitable for children. The publisher is not responsible for changes in content
or website addresses. We advise that Internet searches are supervised by an adult.

CONTENTS

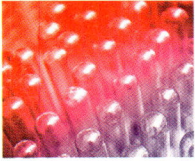

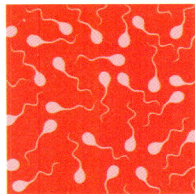

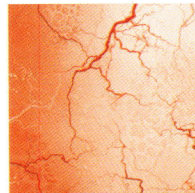

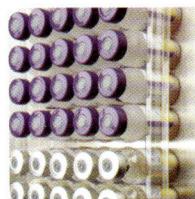

A GLOBAL DISEASE

IN 2007, HIV/AIDS AFFECTED AN ESTIMATED 33 MILLION PEOPLE AROUND THE WORLD, INCLUDING 2 MILLION CHILDREN. THERE WERE 2.7 MILLION NEW INFECTIONS IN THAT YEAR AND 2 MILLION PEOPLE DIED OF AIDS. AFRICA HAS NEARLY 12 MILLION AIDS ORPHANS.

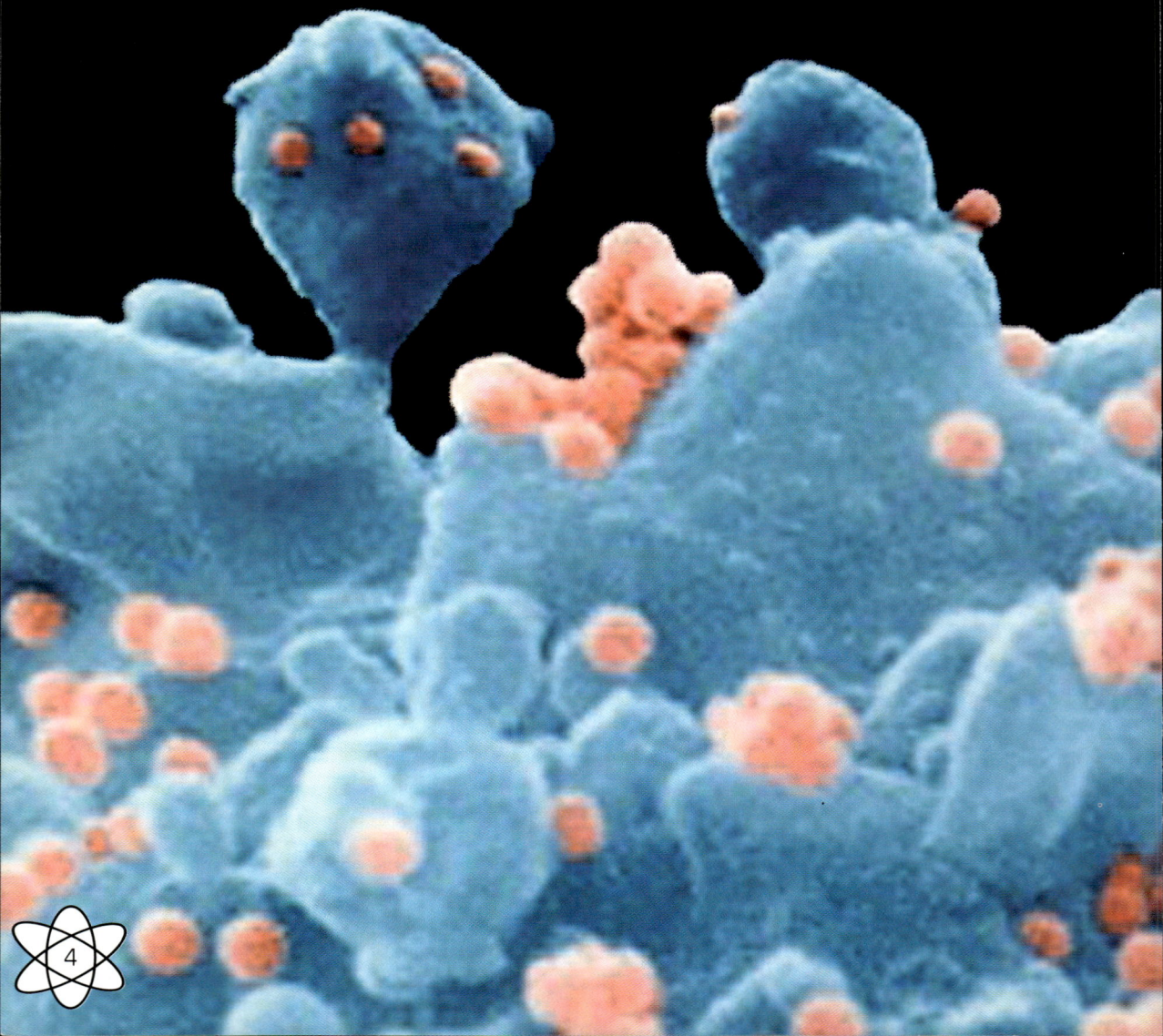

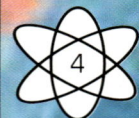

WHAT IS HIV/AIDS?

HIV/AIDS is the name doctors give to an infectious **disease** that has been sweeping the Earth since the early 1980s. HIV stands for 'Human Immunodeficiency **Virus**', which is the **microbe** that causes the disease. AIDS is 'Acquired Immune Deficiency Syndrome', the disease that HIV will eventually cause if left untreated. HIV attacks the body's immune system by invading the T-**cells** that are an essential part of the system. Over a period of several years, these cells are destroyed by the virus and the **immune** system breaks down, leaving the body prey to many different infections and cancers that may eventually prove fatal. However, there are now anti-viral treatments available that can keep HIV in check, so someone who is infected can live with the virus for many years without developing AIDS. Science has a lot to offer in the control of HIV/AIDS. This is a preventable disease, but it is also a global emergency in need of widespread and prompt action to help those affected.

This coloured micrograph shows the surface of a T-cell that is infected with HIV, giving it a lumpy appearance. Small, rounded virus particles (shown in red) cluster on the surface.

WHAT IS A VIRUS?

There are four main types of micro-organisms that cause disease – bacteria, fungi, protozoa and viruses.

All micro-organisms are invisible to the naked eye but the virus is the smallest of all. The diameter of a virus is only 15–300 nanometres (a nanometre is one thousand-millionth of a metre). Viruses cause diseases. These may be minor, such as colds and warts, or more serious and even life-threatening, such as Ebola fever, **SARS**, H1N1 swine flu, AIDS and certain types of cancer.

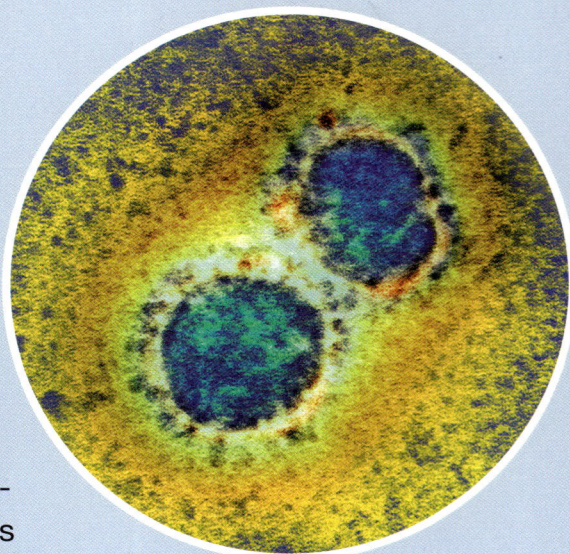

The two blue circles are SARS virus particles. SARS is 'severe acute respiratory syndrome', a fatal lung disease that first appeared in China in 2002.

VIRUSES AND HOSTS

Viruses do not have a life of their own in the way other micro-organisms do. They can only survive inside the cells of a **host** organism, which may be a human, another animal or a plant. Viruses are tiny particles of varying size and shape. All of them have a central core of **genetic** material – either **DNA** (deoxyribonucleic acid) or **RNA** (ribonucleic acid). These may or may not be surrounded by a coat made of **protein**. A virus enters its host in several possible ways – in dirty food or water, or in the aerosol made when someone coughs or sneezes. When it enters cells, the virus can

make many copies of itself that are then released and go on to invade neighbouring cells. The presence of a virus may damage or even kill cells, and this gives rise to disease. Viruses also activate the immune system, which aims to protect the body from micro-organisms.

FIGHTING A VIRUS

There are fewer drugs against viruses than against bacteria. **Antibiotics** only kill bacteria – they do not work against viruses. The best way to prevent viral infections is through **vaccination**, which prepares the immune system for a viral attack taking place.

The flying fox, or fruitbat, is a common sight in Malaysia. Its saliva has been shown to be infected with the Nipah virus (see box right). The Nipah virus can be fatal if it is passed on to humans.

INVESTIGATING THE EVIDENCE: THE VIRUS HUNTERS

The investigation: Scientists tracked down the Nipah virus that in 2004 killed several people in separate outbreaks in Bangladesh and Malaysia. They wanted to find out how viruses were causing new types of infection in humans.

The scientists: Dr Jon Epstein and Dr Peter Daszak from the Consortium for Conservation Medicine, an alliance of top US universities, the US Wildlife Health Center and the Wildlife Trust based in New York, USA.

Collecting the evidence: The scientists visited the remote volcanic island of Pulau Tioman, west of Borneo and 240 km from the Malaysian outbreak of Nipah infection. They were looking for flying foxes, suspected of being the source of the infection. They caught ten or more and took samples of blood and saliva to study in a bio-containment laboratory on the mainland.

The conclusion: Nipah virus was found in the bats' saliva. The Malaysian outbreaks happened near pig farms. The bats feed in fruit trees and infected fruit could have contaminated pig feed. Infected pigs then passed the disease on to humans. Most new diseases, including AIDS, probably come from animals.

CHAPTER ONE

HIV AND HUMANS

HIV BELONGS TO A GROUP OF VIRUSES CALLED **RETROVIRUSES.** THEIR GENETIC MATERIAL IS MADE OF RNA, NOT DNA. LIKE ALL VIRUSES, HIV MAKES COPIES OF ITSELF INSIDE THE CELL, BUT TO DO SO IT NEEDS TO USE AN **ENZYME** CALLED REVERSE TRANSCRIPTASE. THE ABILITY THAT HIV HAS TO COPY ITSELF CAN BE TURNED AGAINST IT BY THE DRUGS THAT ARE USED TO TREAT HIV.

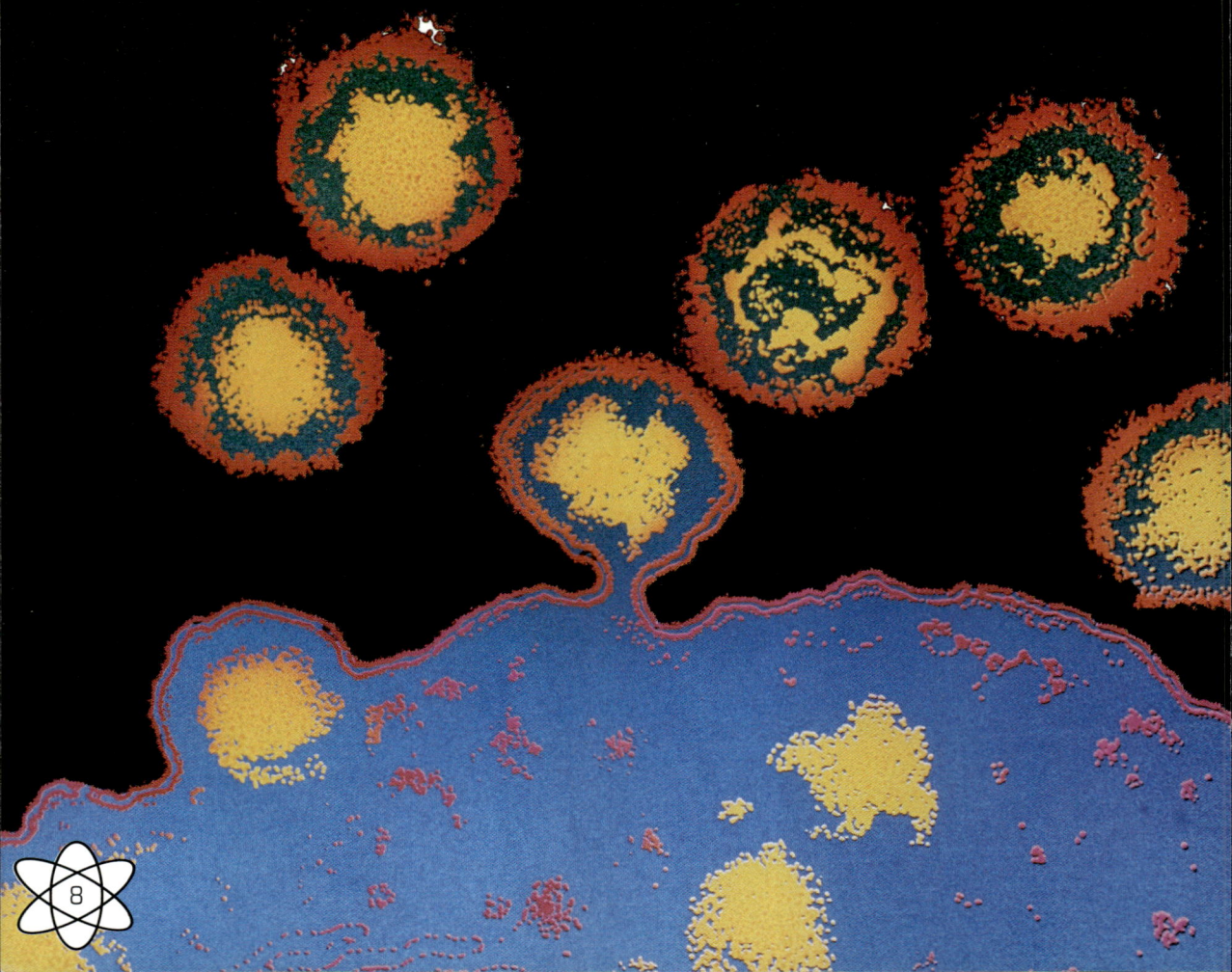

FIRST CONTACT

Once the HIV virus has entered the body, it infects cells known as CD4 cells (also called T4 lymphocytes or helper T-cells), so-called because there are **molecules** of a protein called CD4 displayed on their surface. CD4 is a **receptor** – it acts as a signal and entry point for traffic in and out of the

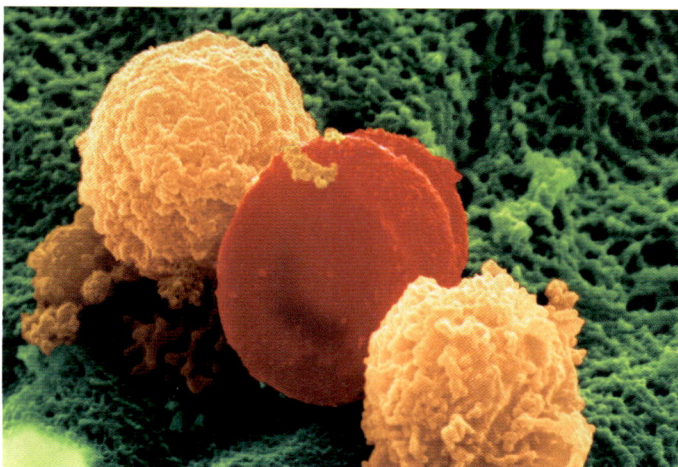

White blood cells (here coloured yellow) are an important part of the body's immune system. They act to protect the body against infection, either by attacking or making antibodies.

cell. The CD4 cells form part of the immune system, which protects the body against infection. In fact, CD4 cells are so important that they are sometimes called the 'conductor' of the 'immune orchestra'. They have the first contact with invading bacteria or viruses, such as HIV, and they alert the other types of immune cell to respond to the threat.

INSIDE THE CELL

The surface of the HIV virus particle is covered with molecules of a protein called Gp120, which helps the virus to get inside the CD4 cells. Gp120 attaches to the

CD4 molecules on the surface of the host cell, using it as a handhold. Once inside the cell, the protein coat of the HIV virus detaches and the RNA heads for the control centre or **nucleus** of the cell. Once there, it takes over the cell's machinery – like all viruses, HIV is a **parasite** – and forces it to make more copies of the virus. These eventually burst out of the cell and go on to infect more cells. The CD4 cell is either damaged or dies. The gradual destruction of a key component of the immune system is what leads to the symptoms of AIDS (and how the disease gets its name).

AIDS viruses (yellow and orange) bud out of a human T-cell. They will now travel through the body, damaging the immune system and exposing it to infection.

SIGNS AND SYMPTOMS

It can take ten years or more between first being infected with HIV and developing AIDS. At first, the body's immune system fights back against the infection and the person appears to be healthy. Despite this, they could still infect other people. Eventually, their immune system breaks down and many different medical problems can occur. However, with treatment, someone with HIV may be able to keep themselves in reasonable health.

Doctors keep track of the progression of HIV infection with two tests – a viral load test, which shows how much virus is in the blood, and a CD4 count (above), which shows how many CD4 cells are left. As the infection progresses, viral load goes up and CD4 count goes down.

THE FOUR STAGES

Doctors divide HIV infection into four stages. The first stage is called HIV infection or seroconversion and lasts from first exposure to the appearance of **antibodies** in the person's blood. This may take up to three months. Antibodies can bind onto viruses and bacteria and help destroy them. Some people get symptoms such as a feverish illness, sore throat or headache soon after they have been infected with HIV. This is a sign of the immune system fighting the infection. The second stage is known as the asymptomatic phase of infection. HIV is a 'silent' infection and there are few, if any, symptoms in this phase, which can last for as long as 15 years. In the third stage, the immune system finally begins to show the signs of damage done to it by HIV. In the fourth and final stage, which many doctors classify as AIDS, the virus becomes more active than before and there are many symptoms such as night sweats, weight loss and diarrhoea. There are also many opportunistic infections, such as pneumocystic carinii (a kind of pneumonia), candida (a yeast infection affecting the mouth) and herpes simplex (cold sores). Various cancers, such as Kaposi's sarcoma, may also occur because the immune system plays a role in protection. AIDS, in its final stages, may also affect the brain, causing **dementia**, a gradual deterioration in faculties.

One symptom of the damage done to the immune system by HIV can be swollen **lymph glands**, which happens in the third stage.

A CAREER IN SCIENCE

Ash Taylor works as a biomedical scientist in the laboratory at Ninewells Hospital in Dundee.

A DAY IN THE LIFE OF …

Biomedical scientists play an important role in healthcare. They carry out a wide range of laboratory tests – often using sophisticated instruments – on human samples that include blood and other types of tissue. They tend to specialize in a particular area. For example, in public health laboratories, they help to investigate outbreaks of diseases such as food poisoning or swine flu. Biomedical scientists in forensic science do laboratory work that helps to catch criminals. The biomedical scientist in immunology, such as those in Ninewells Hospital, specializes in work on the body's immune system. He or she looks at a wide range of medical problems including infectious diseases, parasitic infestations, allergies, tumour growth, tissue grafts and organ transplants.

THE SCIENTIST SAYS …

"Our work is particularly important in the monitoring and treatment of AIDS. We are responsible for turning round the viral load and CD4 counting tests, handling and managing the blood samples, and reporting the results. The machines used to carry out the tests are usually automated, eliminating human error from the results."

Joining a self-help group may give someone the emotional and practical support that they need to tell their loved ones about their HIV infection.

LIVING WITH HIV/AIDS

Living with HIV means living with uncertainty and learning to deal with it. Thanks to a better understanding of the disease and drugs that can treat it, there are now many long-term survivors of HIV/AIDS. In some respects, living with HIV is similar to living with other chronic illnesses such as diabetes, cancer, or heart disease. In other ways, it is different because HIV is a disease that still attracts stigma and prejudice.

From the moment they are given their diagnosis, an HIV positive person faces challenges in many areas of their life. They do not know if or when they will become ill, if they will be able to carry on at work or education, how their finances will work and what their life expectancy will be. People with HIV need to have medical tests every few months to monitor their viral load and CD4 counts. If they are on medication, they will have a lot of different pills to take on a strict timing schedule. They will also have to do all they can to take care of themselves with a good diet, exercise and plenty of rest. Some find that complementary therapies, such as yoga, meditation and aromatherapy, can help them cope.

Some HIV/AIDS sufferers find complementary therapies such as aromatherapy helpful.

CONFIDING IN OTHERS

A big issue in living with HIV is who to tell, when to tell them – and how. This can be especially important if someone needs time off work, college or school. In many countries, people with disabilities – including HIV infection – are protected from job discrimination as long as they can still do the essential part of their work. But there is always a danger of prejudice and rejection. Some fear that they may become infected if they do not really know how the virus is transmitted, or they may judge someone if they think they got the virus through gay sex or drug-taking. It can be especially hard to tell parents, children and other family members about a diagnosis of HIV.

INVESTIGATING THE EVIDENCE: BEING INFECTED BY HIV

The investigation: Doctors wanted to find out why some people avoid getting infected with HIV, even though they have been exposed to the virus.

The scientists: Dr Bill Paxton and Dr Yaoxing Huang at the Aaron Diamond AIDS Research Center in New York, USA, and Dr Steve O'Brien at the National Institutes of Health.

Collecting the evidence:
When HIV was mixed with the CD4 cells of resistant individuals in a test tube, no infection took place. The DNA was analyzed and showed mutations in the CCR5, the 'second receptor' on the CD4 molecule that had been recently discovered. Those that were resistant did not have CCR5 on the surface of their CD4 cells. Further DNA tests estimated that around one per cent of the population of northern Europe have inherited two copies of the **mutated** CCR5 gene – one from their father, one from their mother. These genes should be resistant to HIV infection.

The conclusion: If CD4 is the handhold for HIV, then CCR5 is the foothold. Without CCR5, HIV cannot enter the host cell and the person will not get infected.

CHAPTER TWO

A NEW DISEASE HITS THE WORLD

SCIENTISTS BELIEVE THAT THE **AIDS** EPIDEMIC BEGAN IN THE 1970S OR EVEN EARLIER. IT WAS NOT UNTIL THE 1980S THAT THEY REALIZED THAT A NEW DISEASE HAD EMERGED. THE FIRST CASES REPORTED WERE IN THE USA, THEN IN EUROPE AND AFRICA. BY THE END OF 1986, THERE WERE NEARLY 40,000 KNOWN CASES WORLDWIDE.

ADVENT OF AIDS

Kaposi's sarcoma (KS) is a rare kind of skin cancer, so doctors were surprised when in just one year, 1981, eight cases were found among young homosexual men in New York. At the same time, there was a sudden increase in cases of the lung infection Pneumocystis carinii pneumonia (PCP) in both Los Angeles and New York. The **CDC** (US Centers for Disease Control and Prevention) formed a Task Force to investigate.

At first, it was believed that only gay men were at risk, but cases of PCP were found among drug users and the disease also appeared in the UK. The CDC believed that some underlying disease was causing both KS and PCP but they did not know what it was or how it was transmitted. KS and PCP only occur when the immune system is severely weakened, so it looked as if the new disease was one that undermined immunity. In August 1982, doctors began to call the disease AIDS.

Around this time, doctors in Uganda began to see cases of a new and fatal wasting disease that they called 'slim'. In Zambia and Zaire, there were reports of a very aggressive form of KS. By 1983, it was clear AIDS was global, having been found in the USA, Canada, fifteen European countries, Haiti, Zaire, seven Latin American countries, Australia and Japan.

This coloured x-ray shows the lungs of a patient with advanced Kaposi's sarcoma. The disease begins as lesions on the skin but may spread to internal organs.

DISCOVERY OF THE HIV VIRUS

The race was now on to find the cause of HIV. In a short time, scientists in France and the USA claimed to have isolated a new retrovirus from the blood of AIDS patients. This meant that a test for infection could be developed. Researchers were also hopeful that they would soon develop drugs and a vaccine to fight AIDS.

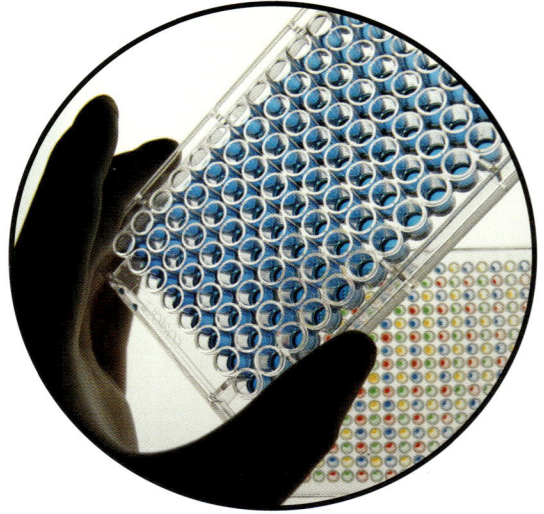

This sample tray is used for the ELISA blood test (see box right), which checks for the presence of proteins that are produced in response to disease-causing organisms.

EUREKA?

In May 1983, virologist Luc Montagnier at the Pasteur Institute in Paris reported the discovery of LAV (lymphadenopathy-associated virus). The scientists sent a sample of the virus to the Centers for Disease Control (CDC) in the USA for further study. A year later, CDC scientist Robert Gallo announced the discovery of a virus, called HTLV-III, that the scientists claimed to be the cause of AIDS. HTLV stands for human T-cell leukaemia/lymphoma virus – a family of viruses that causes cancer. Gallo's team found HTLV-III in the CD4 cells of more than 50 patients who had AIDS and also in some healthy individuals who were at high risk of developing the disease. They found antibodies against the virus

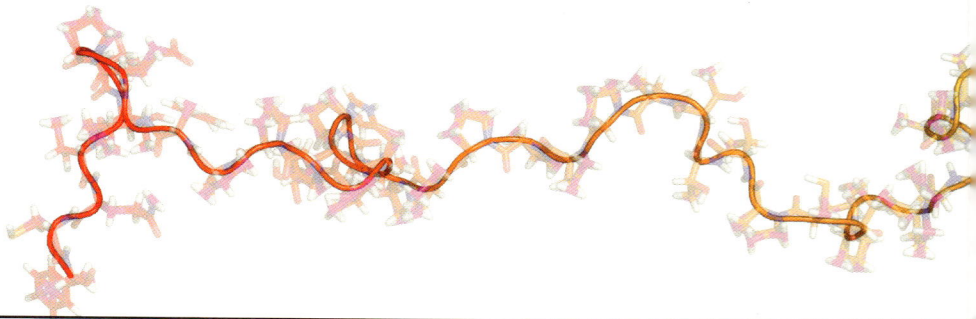

in healthy individuals who were at high risk of developing the disease. They also found antibodies against the virus in the blood of infected people and developed a method for growing the viruses in cells, so that further experiments could be done. There was some controversy over whether Gallo's HTLV-III had come from the LAV sample that Montagnier had sent to the USA. Who was the first to discover the virus that was later called HIV? Later, the French and USA team agreed that LAV and HTLV-III was one and the same virus.

This is a model of a protein produced by a human T-cell leukaemia virus, which causes several diseases.

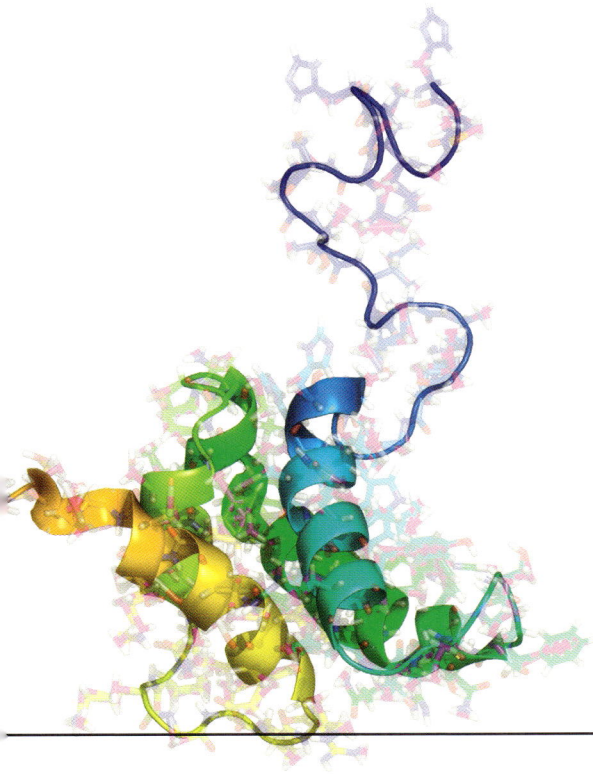

INVESTIGATING THE EVIDENCE: LOOKING FOR ANTIBODIES

The investigation: Scientists aimed to demonstrate that a blood test for HIV can detect the virus in large numbers of blood samples.

The scientists: Robert Gallo and his team at the National Cancer Institute, New York, USA and scientists at other US centres.

Collecting the evidence: A test called an ELISA (Enzyme-Linked ImmunoSorbent Assay) looks for antibodies to HIV in blood samples. If the antibody is present, a colour signal is detected. The test can be semi-automated, with a robot arm doing much of the work of dispensing samples and mixing them with the test reagent. In this investigation, a total of 1,236 blood samples was analyzed between April and September, 1984. In a sub-group of 297 volunteer blood donors, only one per cent gave a positive test. In a sub-group of 88 known AIDS patients, 72 gave a positive antibody result. People with illnesses other than AIDS, such as hepatitis and leukaemia, tested negative in the HIV antibody test. All the test results were confirmed by a second test.

The conclusion: The ELISA test for HIV antibodies is now the basis for HIV diagnosis the world over. A positive result is usually confirmed by a more recent test for the virus itself.

Adult prevalence (%)
- 15.0% – 28.0%
- 5.0% – <15.0%
- 1.0% – <5.0%
- 0.5% – <1.0%
- 0.1% – <0.5%
- <0.1%
- No data available

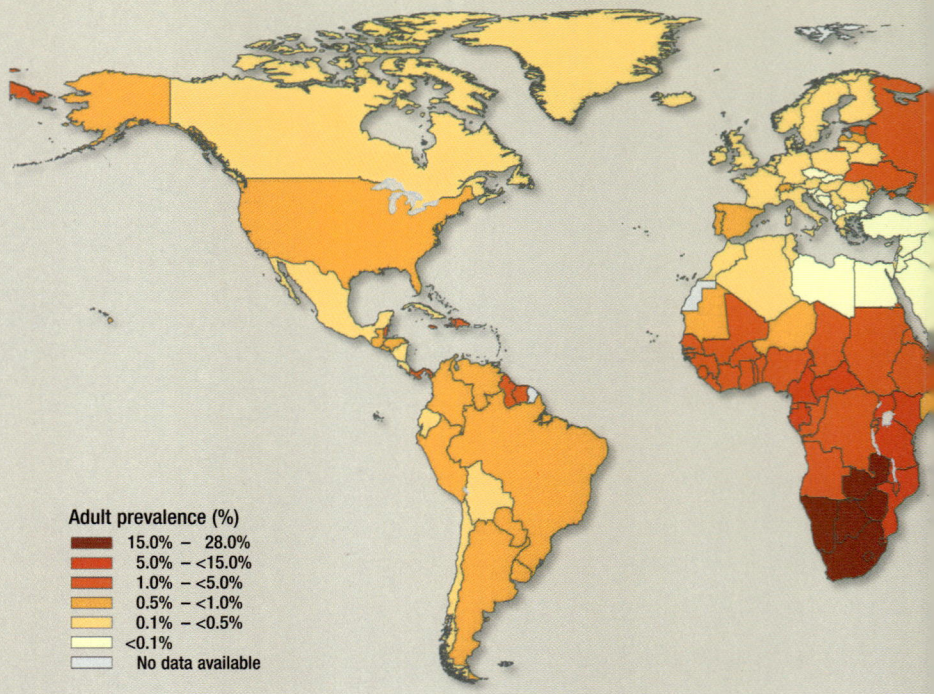

Around 33 million people in the world live with HIV/AIDS. As this 2008 map shows, some countries have a far higher prevalence (total number of cases) than others.

A GROWING EPIDEMIC

Our understanding of HIV/AIDS has grown slowly. Because it is now understood how the disease is transmitted, prevention measures can be taken and some effective drugs that can help people keep HIV infection under control. But a vaccine is not yet available. All of this means that the disease has run ahead of what scientists, governments and the public can do to beat it. No one could have predicted this in the beginning, but today it has become obvious that HIV has the power to change the course of human history.

ACCELERATION

At the end of 1985, when the first HIV test became available, there were nearly 20,000 cases of AIDS around the world, of which 16,000 were in the USA and just 275 in the UK. Many more people were infected than this but testing was not widespread at the time. The **WHO** (World Health Organization) began to collect statistics and their

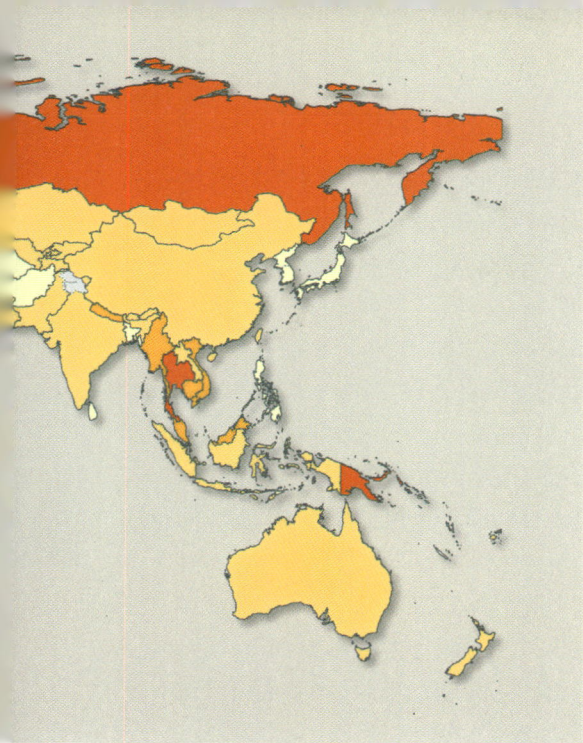

scientists said, at the end of 1986, that they believed up to ten million people worldwide could be HIV positive. By the end of the decade, there were 307,000 recorded cases of AIDS worldwide and this had risen to half a million by the end of 1991. By the end of 1995, the total number of cases was 1.2 million and experts were predicting 40 million HIV infections by 2000. The actual figure that year was 34.3 million.

The HIV/AIDS **epidemic** has slowed a little in the last year or so. There are 33 million people living with HIV/AIDs, including 2 million children. The Joint UN Programme on HIV/AIDS warns that the end of the fight against HIV/AIDS is not yet in sight – there are 2 million people a year dying of the disease.

INVESTIGATING THE EVIDENCE: WHERE DID HIV COME FROM?

The investigation: Through their work, scientists established that the 'ancestor' of HIV is present in wild chimpanzees living in southern Cameroon, Africa.

The scientists: Paul Sharp of the University of Nottingham in the UK and colleagues in Cameroon and at the University of Alabama in Birmingham, USA.

Collecting the evidence: A virus from chimps called SIVcpz (Simian Immunodeficiency Virus) had been thought to be the source of HIV/AIDS but was found in captive animals. In 2006, researchers found the virus in the droppings of wild chimps collected from the floor of the forest in remote areas of jungle. They already knew the genetic sequences they were looking for. It is thought that the first cases of HIV may have occurred as long ago as 1930. The virus mutated to become more dangerous and easily spread – leading to today's **pandemic**.

The conclusion: This study is an important part of the AIDS puzzle, but many questions remain, such as why the chimps do not get sick and how HIV evolved to undermine the human immune system, and are there other animal HIV reservoirs?

FINDING A TREATMENT

Antibiotics, such as penicillin and erthyromycin, have proved their worth against bacterial infections. Viral infections had proved far harder to treat with drugs, although vaccines were known to be effective against infections such as measles, polio and had even helped eradicate smallpox from the planet. So researchers pursued both drugs and vaccines against HIV.

AZT AND AIDS

Azidothymidine (AZT, later known as zidovudine) had been made in 1964 as a possible anti-cancer drug. Scientists at the National Cancer Institute began to see the possibility of using it as a treatment for AIDS. Encouraged by the fact that it worked in the test tube, they went on to test it on patients. After a trial, AZT became the first approved treatment for AIDS. It does not destroy HIV, but it keeps it in check. In 1989, researchers showed that AZT slows progression to AIDS in HIV-positive people who had no

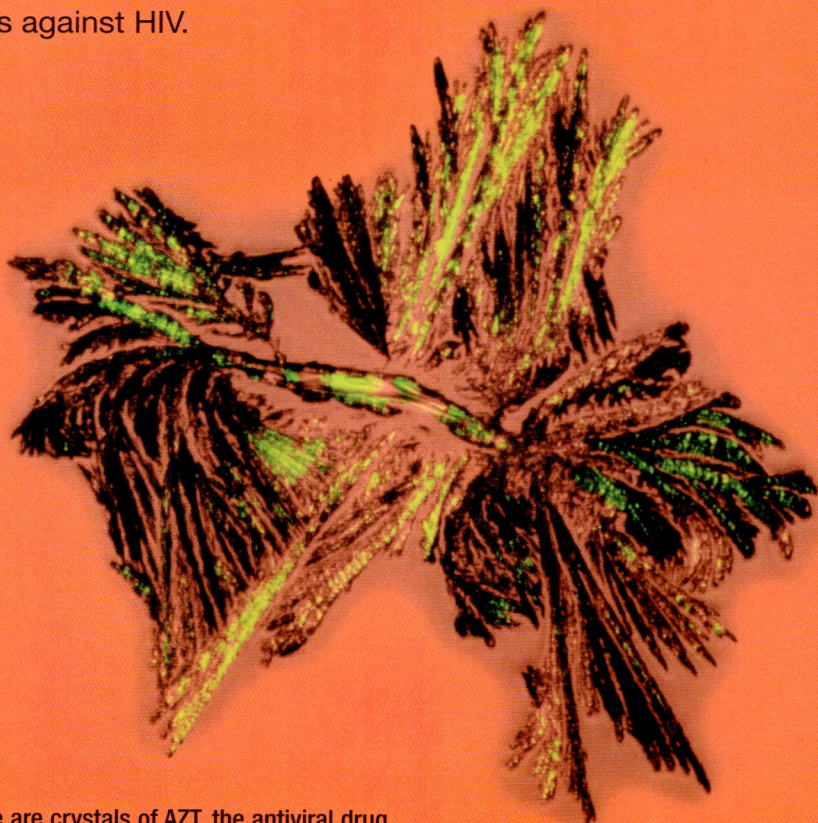

These are crystals of AZT, the antiviral drug that is being used to treat patients with AIDS.

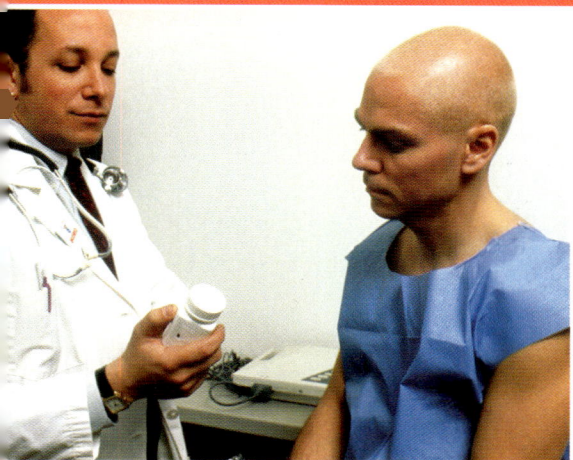

A doctor treats an HIV-positive patient with AZT during a trial before it was approved.

symptoms. However, AZT is not an ideal drug – it has many side-effects, including **anaemia**.

COMBINATION DRUGS

In 1989, dideoxyinosine (ddl) was discovered, followed by a related drug called dideoxycytosine (ddC). Together, ddC and AZT proved to work better than either drug alone. This was the start of the combination therapy that is used today to prevent and treat AIDS. AZT also reduces the risk of transmitting HIV from mother to baby at a very low level. Unfortunately, a few years ago it became obvious that HIV can mutate to become resistant to the drugs used to keep it under control. Today, scientists are working to create new drugs that can overcome this problem.

INVESTIGATING THE EVIDENCE: DOES AZT REDUCE THE RISK OF DYING FROM AIDS?

The investigation: An initial trial showed that AZT was safe to give to patients and that it increased CD4 counts. This set the scene for a larger investigation to see if AZT could prevent people dying from AIDS.

The scientists: A team from the US National Cancer Institute (NCI) joined with researchers from the Burroughs Wellcome Foundation in North Carolina, USA, who had discovered AZT.

Collecting the evidence: The researchers gave 145 patients with AIDS tablets of AZT every four hours for 24 weeks. Another 137 received an inactive 'dummy' tablet called a **placebo** instead of AZT. The trial had to be blind – that is, set up so that no one (researchers, doctors, nurses, patients) knew who was getting AZT and who was on the placebo until the trial was over.

Conclusion: After a few months, it became clear that AZT was having some effect. Only one person died in the AZT group compared to 19 in the placebo group. The trial was stopped early because it was not thought ethical to deny the patients in the placebo group the benefits of AZT. Approved by the US Food and Drug Administration (FDA) on the basis of this investigation, AZT was the first drug to slow the progression of AIDS.

CHAPTER THREE

AIDS IN AFRICA

NUMBERS VARY GREATLY IN AFRICA. IN SOMALIA AND GAMBIA, LESS THAN 2 PER CENT OF THE POPULATION IS INFECTED, WHILE IN SOUTH AFRICA AND ZAMBIA, AROUND 20 PER CENT IS INFECTED. HIV/AIDS IN AFRICA IS COMPLICATED BY OTHER DISEASES, SUCH AS TUBERCULOSIS AND MALARIA. IN AFRICA THERE ARE TWO KINDS OF HIV. THE HIV-1 VIRUS IS THE SAME AS THAT FOUND IN THE USA AND EUROPE, WHILE HIV-2 IS FOUND MAINLY IN WEST AFRICA. FORTUNATELY, HIV-2 IS HARDER TO TRANSMIT.

VULNERABLE

In Africa, HIV is more likely to be transmitted by heterosexual (man/woman) than homosexual (man/man or woman/woman) sex. And because the blood supply is not as safe as in Europe and the USA, transmission of HIV through **blood transfusion** may happen. There is also a much higher rate of mother-to-baby HIV transmission. Mothers may not know they are HIV postive, because they do not have access to testing, or the drugs that could stop this may not be readily available.

The time it takes for HIV infection to progress to AIDS is about the same in all countries. But infectious diseases are more common in Africa, so the infected person may get ill more quickly. Poverty and malnutrition make it harder for some Africans to fight the disease. Tuberculosis is the most common opportunistic infection to affect those with HIV in Africa. Because it is highly **contagious**, other people are put at risk. Children with malaria are at risk from HIV because they may receive a blood transfusion for anaemia. Malaria reduces the number of red cells in the blood, so a person becomes weak and anaemic. AIDS in Africa is often called 'slim' disease because the sick person seems to waste away.

Children are particularly vulnerable in sub-Saharan Africa, and many of them are left orphaned because of AIDS.

Children who have lost their parents are usually put in an orphanage. If an orphan is HIV-positive or has had parents who have died of AIDS, they are often discriminated against and may not be allowed in school. They become isolated in their society.

HIV AND CHILDREN IN AFRICA

At the end of 2007, there were two million children living with HIV around the world. Most were infected by their mother at birth and more than 90 per cent of them are in Africa. Over 15 million children around the world (11.4 million in sub-Saharan Africa) under the age of eighteen had lost one or more of their patients to AIDS by the end of 2007.

AIDS AND CHILDREN

Already, 1.4 million children in South Africa have lost at least one parent to the disease, and the number is around one million per country in Nigeria, Zimbabwe, Uganda and Tanzania. Of these, 15 per cent are under the age of 4, 35 per cent are between 5 and 9, and half are between 10 and 15. The pain of losing a parent to AIDS starts long before death for these children. They are neglected because the parent is not able to

▶ ▶ www.unicef.org/aids/index_action.html

care for them in the way they would want to. Not only does the child go short on food and the other things that money buys, they also do not get the usual affection and attention they would expect from their mother or father. They may end up looking after a sick parent, which means they miss out on school. Often, if one parent is HIV-positive the other one is too, so there may be more than one sick person to nurse. Education is essential to help a child fight against the damage that AIDS has done to his or her life.

Children with HIV/AIDS themselves need a lot of support from relatives. They also need medical treatment and education.

A CAREER IN SCIENCE

Dr Refanus Kooper is the Chief of the ART (anti-retroviral therapy) Clinic at Katutura State Hospital, Windhoek, in Namibia, Africa.

A DAY IN THE LIFE OF …

Dr Kooper's team, which first provided treatment in 2003, takes on 80 to 120 new patients a month for ART. They are currently looking after about 5,000 adults and 1,100 children at the clinic on a regular basis. Nurses from the clinic go out into schools in Katatura to talk and educate people about HIV and to tell them that they can come to the clinic for testing. Apart from ART, the doctors and nurses at the clinic also do cervical smears, family planning, TB screening and counselling. They try to help patients with problems such as food security – making sure that people do not live in hunger or fear of starvation. It is a busy life – particularly because the clinic is very short of doctors and nurses.

THE SCIENTIST SAYS …

"I am just grateful that we started this programme and that we could base our start on World Health Organization guidelines. Working from the guidelines, we are able to help our patients and give them quality care. Our motto is 'Excellence is our belief, but to see a smile on a patient's face is our pride.' "

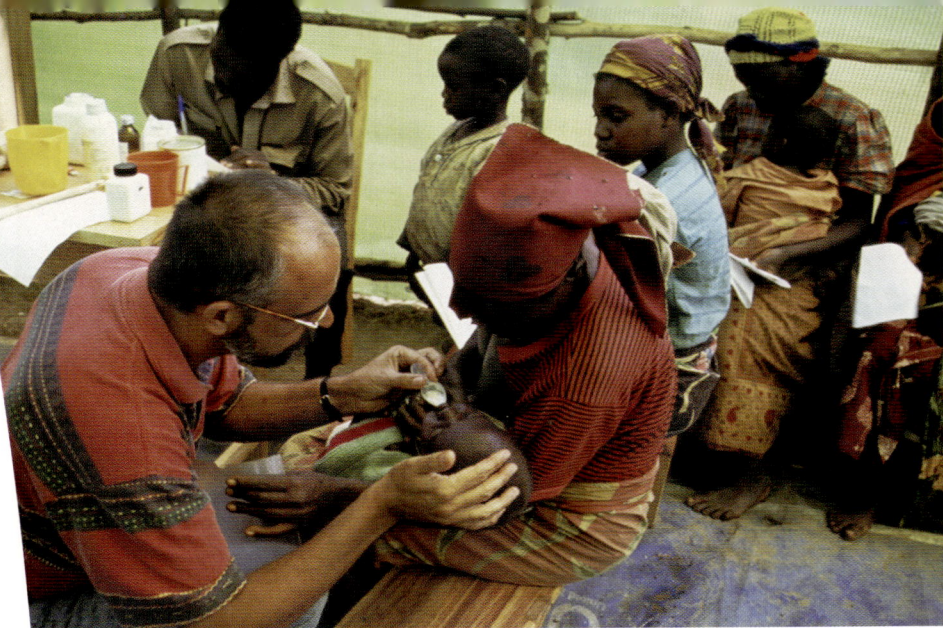

Caring for families affected by HIV/AIDS places new, and sometimes overwhelming, demands on healthcare clinics in Africa.

DEALING WITH AIDS IN AFRICA

There are certain things that have to be done to control the virus. The best way forward is to prevent more cases of HIV/AIDS, which means educating people about how it is transmitted. Condoms can protect from HIV during sexual intercourse by providing a barrier against the passage of the virus from one person to another.

Secondly, people who have already got HIV must be cared for by offering access to testing, treatment and support. If they become ill with AIDS, they need medical care. And support for AIDS goes beyond the individual to help the family and the whole community.

These strategies need a lot of money. To make a real difference, about $10 billion a year needs to be given to the African nations most affected by HIV/AIDS.

A GLOBAL FUND

In 2001, the then UN Secretary General Kofi Annan announced the Global Fund to Fight AIDS, TB and malaria. Anyone around the world can contribute – governments, charities and ordinary people. So far, around 50 nations are involved, many of them the richer countries

www.theglobalfund.org/en/

Demonstrations, like this one in Washington, USA, in 2003, aim to encourage financial support.

but also some of the African nations who are most affected by HIV/AIDS. So far, more than $15 billion has been approved, but only just under half of this has actually reached those who need it. The slow distribution of the Fund's money is a real problem.

The Fund has provided care and support for AIDS orphans, obtained HIV drugs for those who need them and also trained many people in Africa to care for those with HIV/AIDS.

The USA gives about a third of the Global Fund's money but it also has its own Fund, called the President's Emergency Plan for AIDS Relief. It is thought to provide money faster, but is particular about who it helps.

INVESTIGATING THE EVIDENCE: PREVENTION IN SWAZILAND

The investigation: Nearly 40 per cent of the population of Swaziland in Africa is HIV positive. Infant mortality is as high as 91 in 1,000, with half the deaths being due to AIDS. Something has to be done urgently about prevention.

The workers: Thabsile, Simanga and Sindi are 'peer educators'. They are members of Swaziland For Positive Living (SWAPOL), a local organization supported by UNICEF that works in rural communities to provide training and education on HIV/AIDS, positive living and good nutrition advice and care for those who are ill and their families.

The project: The three young workers are all HIV-positive. They go out into churches and community places to educate people about HIV prevention, testing and treatment. They help people face their fears, for instance, that HIV will affect employment. They also give facts – for example, that traditional medicines will not work against HIV and modern drugs are needed.

The conclusion: With young people like this sharing their experiences and living positively, others begin to see that HIV is not a death sentence and that a full life can still lie ahead.

CHAPTER FOUR

AIDS AROUND THE WORLD

THE CRISIS CONTINUES TO GROW. OF THE 33 MILLION PEOPLE WHO ARE LIVING WITH HIV/AIDS, MANY WILL DIE WITHIN THE NEXT 20 YEARS. NEARLY 3 MILLION PEOPLE AROUND THE WORLD WERE NEWLY INFECTED IN 2005. AIDS HAS HAD ITS WORST IMPACT IN AFRICA, BUT THERE IS NO COUNTRY IN THE WORLD THAT IS NOT AFFECTED IN SOME WAY BY THE DISEASE.

AIDS SPREADS

In Asia, where half of the world's population lives, AIDS arrived later than in Africa. By 2007, 5 million people were living with HIV/AIDS. It is hard to be certain about these numbers, because some countries do not yet have good ways of recording cases of the disease. The Asian epidemic has begun to spread from high-risk groups, such as injecting drug users and sex workers, to the general population.

In Eastern Europe and Central Asia, HIV/AIDS has increased rapidly – from 1.2 million cases in 2003 to 1.5 million in 2007 – largely from injecting drug use.

In some of the Caribbean island states, there are some of the worst HIV/AIDS outbreaks outside sub-Saharan Africa, with unprotected heterosexual sex the main cause. Both sex and drug use seem to be fuelling HIV/AIDS in Latin America, where there were 140,000 new infections in 2007. In the USA and western Europe, the problem continues. In the UK, for example, more than one quarter of new cases in 2004 were among women. This suggests that heterosexual sex is still an important cause of HIV, despite prevention work.

Medical technicians at the Research Institute for Tropical Medicine in Manila in the Philippines carry out tests for viruses including HIV/AIDS and dengue fever.

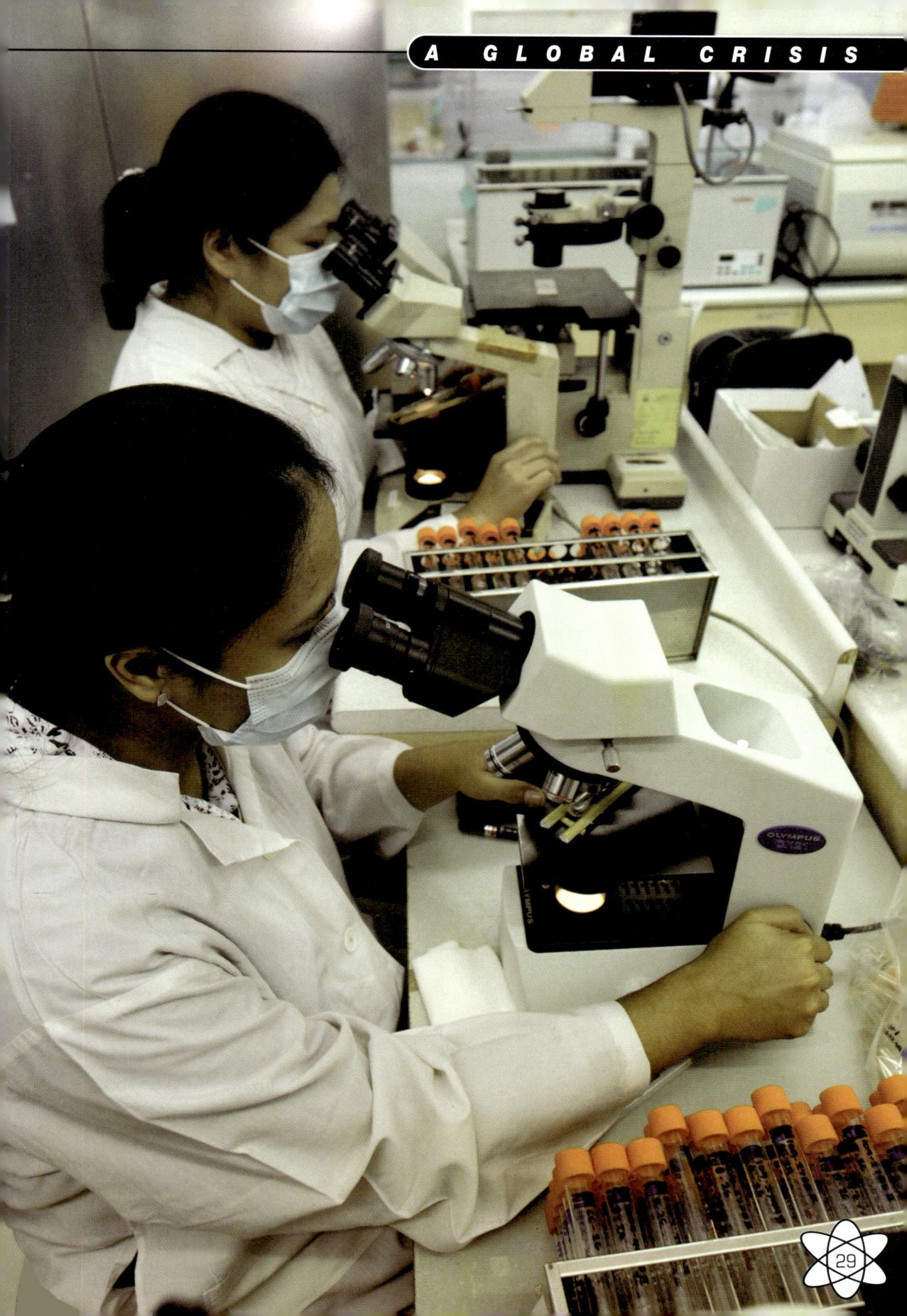

SPOTLIGHT ON THE CARIBBEAN

After Africa, the Caribbean island states are the worst affected by HIV/AIDS. Cases in Haiti came to light as early as the 1980s and the country still has the highest infection rate in the region with 2.2 per cent of the population living with HIV/AIDS. Haiti has long been a country in turmoil, and is an example of how political conflict can worsen public health. HIV in Haiti is mainly transmitted by heterosexual sex with most of the infections and deaths happening among young adults. There has also been a high rate of mother-to-child transmission. It is thought that as many as 200,000 Haitian children have lost one or both parents to AIDS.

MAKING CHANGES

Some governments in the Caribbean are aware of the problems that their people face and are taking action.

In Cuba, for example, there is a widespread testing and prevention programme underway and the infection rate in the country has now gone down to 0.1 per cent. All those who can benefit get free drugs in Cuba. Barbados and Bermuda have also provided drugs to infected people and this has reduced the number of AIDS deaths by a half.

A Haitian boy stands by a sewage canal in the Cité Soleil slum of Port-au-Prince.

A CAREER AS A SUPPORT WORKER

Sorokhaibam Thoibi Devi, or Thoibi as she is called, is General Secretary of the Manipur Network of Positive People (MNP+) in Thoubal, India, and also an 'AIDS widow' with two young children and no family support. She runs income-generation programmes in food preservation, weaving, embroidery and mat-weaving for HIV-positive women.

A DAY IN THE LIFE OF …

Thoibi organizes awareness programmes in Thoubal, encouraging HIV-positive women to accept their status. Largely as a result of her work, MNP+ now has 230 women who are actual members and more than 400 in total that are in contact with the organization. Thoibi has individually approached and persuaded AIDS widows like herself to declare their HIV status, join her network and begin to learn how to live their lives again. One example is Rani who, from selling snacks on the street for a very low wage, has now become an outreach worker and earns a decent living.
Rani has just celebrated her eldest daughter completing high school.

THE SUPPORT WORKER SAYS …

"The fact that I have been able to help other women like me … is what makes me the happiest …. Nothing pleases me more than the fact that I am helping others realize that there is life after HIV/AIDS."

CHAPTER FIVE

HOW HIV IS TRANSMITTED

INFECTIOUS DISEASES CAN BE PASSED FROM ONE PERSON TO ANOTHER. IN THE YEARS FOLLOWING THE DISCOVERY OF THE FIRST CASES OF AIDS, MANY PEOPLE WERE VERY FRIGHTENED THAT THEY MIGHT CATCH THE DISEASE. TODAY, WE KNOW A LOT MORE AND PEOPLE CAN FIND OUT ABOUT THE RISKS OF BECOMING INFECTED WITH HIV AND WHAT TO DO TO PREVENT IT.

'CATCHING' HIV

Micro-organisms lurk in food, water, on people's skin and in blood, as well as in animals such as mosquitoes. This means that there are many different ways in which people can catch an infectious disease. Colds, flu, measles and chicken pox are contagious – they can be caught by everyday contact with other people. HIV is not contagious. It is transmitted mainly through exposure to HIV-infected blood.

The most common way of becoming infected with HIV is having sexual intercourse with a person who is HIV-positive. Another way is by injecting drugs such as heroin with a needle or syringe that has been used by an infected person. HIV can also pass to a newborn baby from an infected mother. But you cannot get HIV/AIDS from kissing, shaking hands, sharing crockery or cutlery, or any other everyday contact with an infected person. We also know that sneezing, coughing, giving blood, mosquito bites, or licking stamps do not transmit HIV. Swimming pools, toilet seats and showers cannot give you HIV either. In other words, although HIV is highly dangerous, it is not very easy to catch.

Princess Diana tried to educate people about HIV/AIDS, at a time when people were afraid to even touch those who had the disease.

People who inject themselves with drugs account for a significant number of HIV infections around the world, usually because they are using infected needles.

SEX, DRUGS AND AIDS

Blood and other body fluids of someone with HIV/AIDS will usually carry the virus. It can enter a person's body through tiny cuts or sores in the **mucous membranes** that line the passages into the human body.

Research has shown that the blood and sexual fluids of a person with HIV/AIDS can contain enough virus to infect someone else. The sexual fluids are semen that is produced by a man and vaginal fluid that is produced by a woman.

SEX, DRUGS

Heterosexual intercourse can lead to infection through the man's semen. It could get inside the woman's bloodstream through any break in the mucous membrane lining the vagina. The man could also become infected if vaginal fluid containing HIV enters his bloodstream through a tiny sore on the penis.

Heterosexual or homosexual sex, where the penis is inserted into the rectum (back passage) through the anus carries an even greater risk of HIV/AIDS. This is because the anus and rectum linings are thinner than that of the vagina and more likely to be broken, so infected semen can enter the bloodstream.

Injecting drugs can also lead to transmission of HIV. The needle or syringe used by someone with HIV/AIDS can contain tiny, invisible, traces of infected blood. If these are shared with someone else, HIV can pass into their bloodstream through the injection. Body piercings and tattoos carry a risk, unless a fresh needle is used on each customer.

Having a tattoo done is a personal choice, but it carries with it the risk of infection.

INVESTIGATING THE EVIDENCE: DO WOMEN TRANSMIT THE VIRUS VIA THE VAGINA?

The investigation: The more we understand about how an infection like HIV spreads, the more effective its prevention can be. One important question is whether, and how, women transmit HIV to men during sex, and whether the virus can pass from the body into the fluids of the woman's cervix and vagina.

The scientists: A team at the University of Washington, Seattle, led by Dr David Clemetson, who has studied infectious diseases in Kenya and New Guinea.

Collecting the evidence: Nearly 100 HIV-positive women attended a clinic for sexually transmitted diseases in Nairobi, Kenya. They voluntarily gave specimens of fluid from the cervix and vagina. These were tested in the lab for HIV DNA. One third of the samples from the cervix came up positive and one sixth of samples from the vagina. Using the contraceptive pill and being pregnant increased the risk of HIV being present in the women's vaginal and cervical fluids.

Conclusion: Some women who are HIV positive will shed the virus into their cervix and vagina. Since there is no way for a man to know if a women is, or is not, shedding the virus, safer sex practice (using a condom) is essential to prevent transmission of the virus during sexual intercourse.

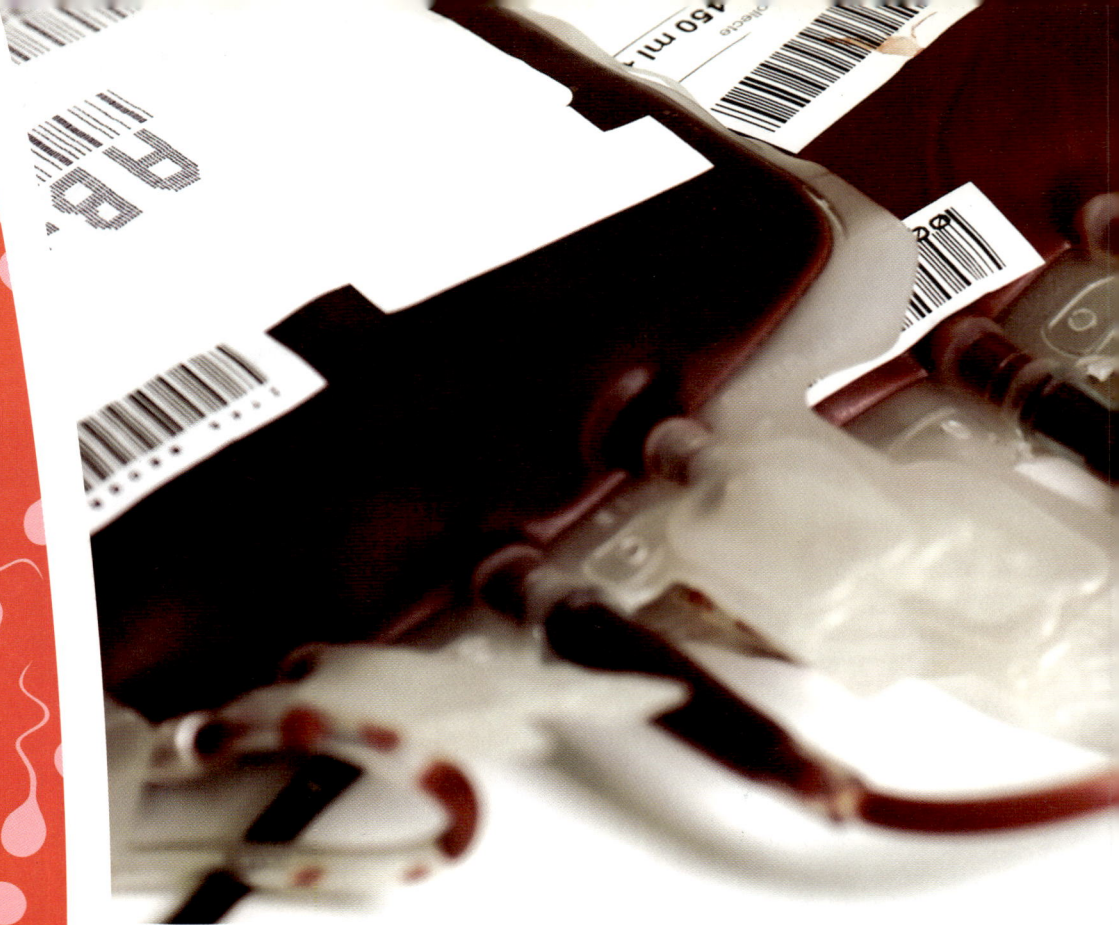

BLOOD AND AIDS

Blood transfusions and organ donations can be life-saving, but they can also transmit viruses. Transmission of HIV through medical treatment is now rare but many people have become infected in this way in the past. There is still a risk of catching HIV if blood is not screened and treated for the virus.

HAEMOPHILIA AND AIDS

In 1982, the CDC reported that a 20-month-old baby had died of AIDS after receiving several blood transfusions. This new case suggested that AIDS was an infectious disease. It also drew attention to safety in blood supply.

People with **haemophilia** are born without one of the proteins that blood needs to **clot** normally. In the 1980s, these clotting factors were made from blood donations. The blood was pooled from 5,000 donors,

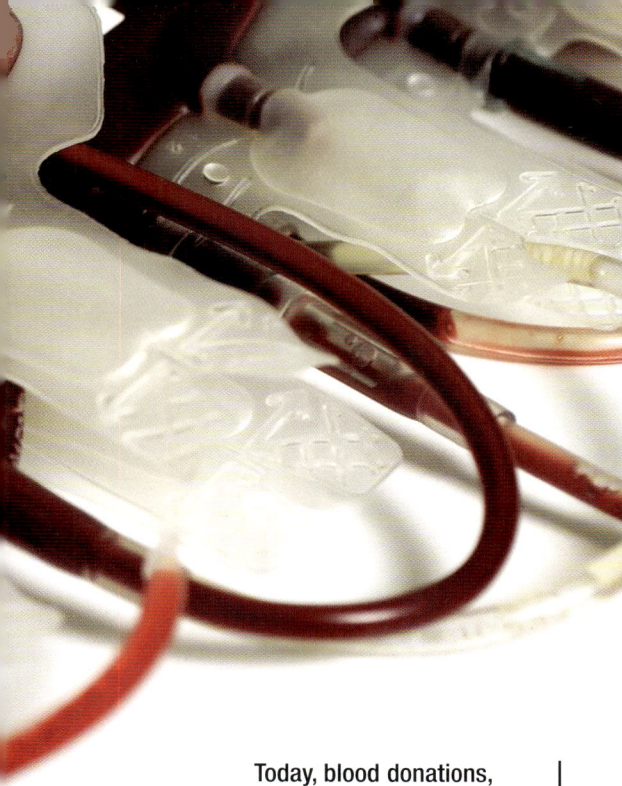

Today, blood donations, also called 'blood products', are carefully screened for infections.

so the risk of being exposed to HIV was much higher than in the rest of the population. People who may have had HIV were warned not to give blood. When a test for HIV was discovered, it was applied to screen blood donations. But this was too late for many. More than half the 17,000 haemophiliacs in the USA became HIV-positive and many died.

Healthcare workers looking after people with HIV/AIDS may also be at risk. They may accidentally stick themselves with a needle that contains infected blood, or get blood splashed into their eye or nose.

A CAREER IN SCIENCE

Marjorie Doty is a certified medical blood bank technician with the American Society for Clinical Pathology and she is the Manager of the Transfusion Medicine Academic Center at Florida Blood Services in St Petersburg, USA.

A DAY IN THE LIFE OF ...

Blood banking is demanding, with unpredictable hours and the heavy responsibility of knowing that just one mismatched unit of blood can cause a patient's death. Every year, an average of 29 million units of blood components are transfused into patients in the USA. These transfusions are made possible by the blood bank technology specialists who have a background in medical laboratory technology as well as additional training in immunohematology. They carry out both routine and advanced testing including HIV testing, to make sure the blood is safe and compatible.

THE SCIENTIST SAYS ...

"Blood bankers receive little recognition for their work and skill because they are not as visible as doctors or nurses. But that's not important. Here, you know that what you've done has helped save a life or got someone through surgery successfully."

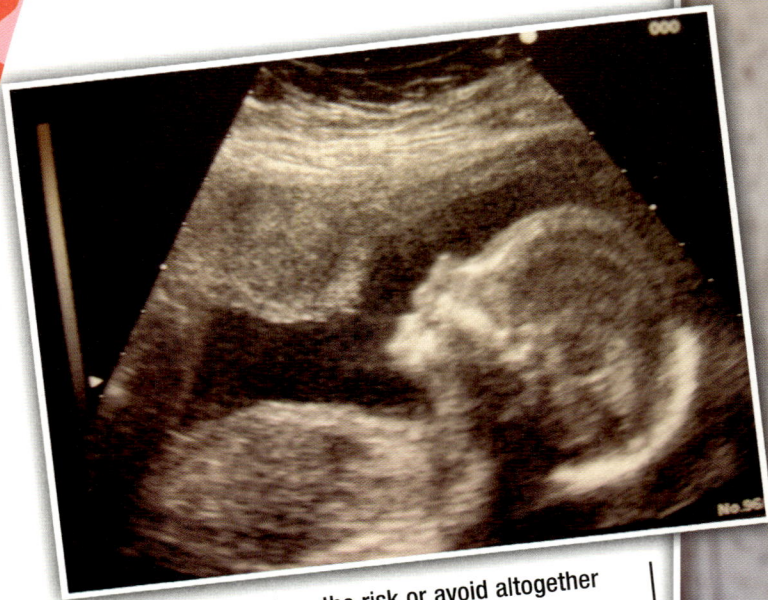

It is possible to reduce the risk or avoid altogether mother-to-child transmission during pregnancy.

MOTHER AND CHILD

An HIV positive mother can pass the virus on to her baby during pregnancy, birth or breastfeeding. If the child is born with HIV, then he or she may develop AIDS within a few years. However, if a woman knows she is HIV positive, there are several ways in which the unborn child can be protected.

Many women who become infected with HIV, whether or not they know about it, become pregnant. The first case of mother-to-child transmission of HIV was discovered by the Center for Disease Control and Prevention in Atlanta, USA, in 1982. Around 15 to 30 per cent of babies born to HIV-positive mothers become infected if they do not receive treatment. Seven out of ten of these infections happen during birth, when the child is exposed to the mother's blood. Breast milk can also contain the HIV virus and another 15 per cent of infections occur in breastfeeding. The risk of infection is greater in mothers with a high level of HIV in their blood or a low CD4 count.

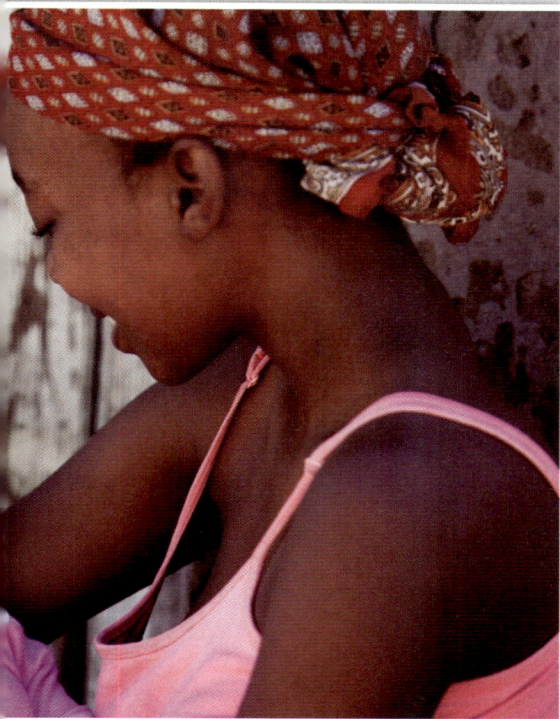

An unborn child can be protected from HIV, but first the mother must realize that she is infected herself.

PROTECTION

In some countries, all pregnant women are screened for HIV, while in others only those at risk are. Mothers can take medication during pregnancy and avoid breastfeeding. Caesarian section (removing the baby from the womb by surgery) helps to reduce the risk of transmission. In the USA and Europe, these measures have reduced the risk to less than two per cent. In developing countries, the rates are higher because mothers cannot get the drugs and may not have alternatives to breastfeeding.

INVESTIGATING THE EVIDENCE: IS NEVIRAPINE A USEFUL ALTERNATIVE?

The investigation: Taking AZT during childbirth can help prevent HIV transmission from an HIV-positive mother to her newborn baby. This study looked at whether nevirapine, a newer anti-HIV drug, could also prevent mother-to-child transmission of HIV.

The scientists: The team was led by Laura Guay, an infectious disease specialist at Johns Hopkins Center for Global Health, in Baltimore, Maryland, USA.

Collecting the evidence: From November 1997 to April 1999, the scientists enrolled 626 HIV-positive pregnant women attending Mulago Hospital in Kampala, Uganda. The women were given either AZT or nevirapine at the onset of, and during, labour. Their babies received the same drug during the first seven days of their lives. The babies were tested for HIV at birth, at age 6–8 weeks and again at 14–16 weeks. At birth, 10.4% of babies on AZT had HIV, compared to 8.2% of those on nevirapine. At eight weeks, the figures were 21.3% and 11.9%, and at 16 weeks, 25.1% and 13.1%.

The conclusion: Nevirapine is more effective than AZT in reducing transmission of HIV from mother to child. This simple and effective treatment could be widely applied in less developed countries.

CHAPTER SIX

EDUCATION AND AWARENESS

EVERYONE NEEDS TO KNOW THE FACTS ABOUT HIV/AIDS. IT CAN ONLY BE PREVENTED IF PEOPLE KNOW WHAT THEY NEED TO DO TO AVOID BEING INFECTED. EDUCATION CAN OVERCOME IGNORANCE AND WRONG IDEAS, BUT TO BE EFFECTIVE, IT HAS TO BE DELIVERED IN THE RIGHT WAY.

AWARENESS OF AIDS

Education does not always have to be given by teachers in a classroom. A doctor's office, clinics – especially those for drug treatment, sexually transmitted diseases and family planning – are places where people can ask questions and be given written information about HIV/AIDS.

The mass media – TV, newspapers, magazines, the internet and poster campaigns – are all good ways of spreading messages about public health. Theatre, music and charity events are also useful. But the message should motivate and empower people, not make them afraid or encourage discrimination.

Theatre, music and charity events are used to educate people about HIV/AIDS. This is the ballroom inside the city hall in Vienna, Austria, during the Life Ball 2009, which is Europe's largest event for the fight against HIV/AIDS. Life Ball began in 1993, and is now very successful at raising awareness.

KEEPING BLOOD SAFE

There is not much that people can do to stop themselves contracting HIV through contaminated blood. They have to rely on their governments and health systems to take action. If these bodies do nothing, campaigners should take action.

However, personal choice can also play an important part in preventing AIDS, as sexual intercourse and drug use are two of the main risk factors. The most effective way of avoiding HIV infection is abstinence – that is, not having sexual intercourse at all and not injecting drugs. For people who are under the age of sexual consent and those who are not long-term drug users, abstinence can be a very good choice.

Another approach is harm reduction – that is accepting that abstinence is difficult, impractical or not a realistic choice. If people are going to have sex or inject drugs then they can be helped to do so in a safer way.

PROTECT YOURSELF

Having fewer sexual partners – or being monogamous (having only one partner) – is a good way of reducing HIV/AIDS risk. When people do have

Personal choices have to be made by individuals and couples, but it is possible to prevent HIV infection.

penetrative sex, then a condom (a disposable rubber sheath that covers the penis during sex) can prevent the transmission of the virus.

Sex education for young people is an important part of HIV prevention. This has to go hand-in-hand with social skills and relationships training, so teenagers feel confident enough to say 'no' to sex if they are not ready for it and to insist on safer sex when they are. For injecting drug users, clinics and organizations can provide clean needles for injection and this will reduce the risk of HIV infection. But needle exchange schemes are controversial because critics think the practice allows users to think it is all right to take illegal drugs.

Both male condoms (below) and female condoms act as barriers to sexually transmitted infections, including HIV/AIDS. They have been shown to reduce infection rates in both men and women.

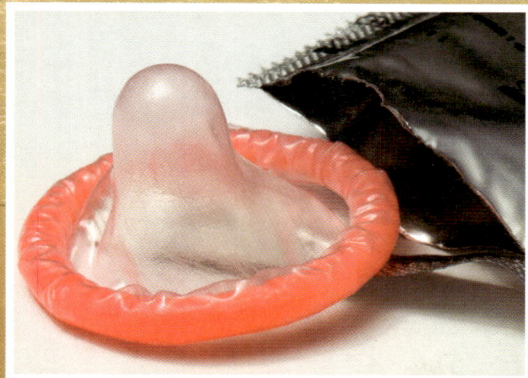

A CAREER AS AN OUTREACH WORKER

Tony Nguyen is the co-ordinator of the Asian and Pacific Islander Wellness Centers MSM (Men who have Sex with Men) programme. He became involved in safer-sex education several years ago as a volunteer.

A DAY IN THE LIFE OF ...

Tony spends a lot of time doing outreach work with the Vietnamese community in the San Francisco Bay area (outreach work tries to reach and involve at risk groups that are not in contact with services already). Sex is taboo in most Asian cultures, so Tony has to break down barriers to even begin a conversation on the subject. He runs workshops on everything from basic safer sex tips to how to admit that you are HIV-positive. He also provides a couples and one-on-one counselling service for those that need it. Tony's main aims are to get people to be safe when engaging in sex and always use condoms.

THE OUTREACH WORKER SAYS ...

"There are so many personal stories, small triumphs I hear about every day from working with people one-on-one that is so satisfying. But there is also so much more work to be done."

A scientist puts a viral solution on the leaf of a cowpea plant in order to infect it. This is part of research to produce a plant vaccine for AIDS being conducted in Norwich, England. The aim is to provoke the plant to produce virus particles for a vaccine.

THE SEARCH FOR A VACCINE

Early vaccines were made with live or weakened forms of a virus. When they enter the body, the immune system makes antibodies and puts T-cells on alert. Today's vaccines are safer. Some are a fragment of DNA from the virus and are totally synthetic. But it has been hard to make an effective vaccine against HIV because the virus attacks cells of the immune system – those that a vaccine would need to activate. HIV also hides away in the nucleus of the cell, where it evades the immune response. It is also able to mutate rapidly, which makes any vaccine less effective. Researchers think that vaccines that have a combined effect – arousing T-cells and making antibodies – are the most effective.

FINDING A SOLUTION

There are around 30 vaccines being tested currently on humans by the International AIDS Vaccine Initiative

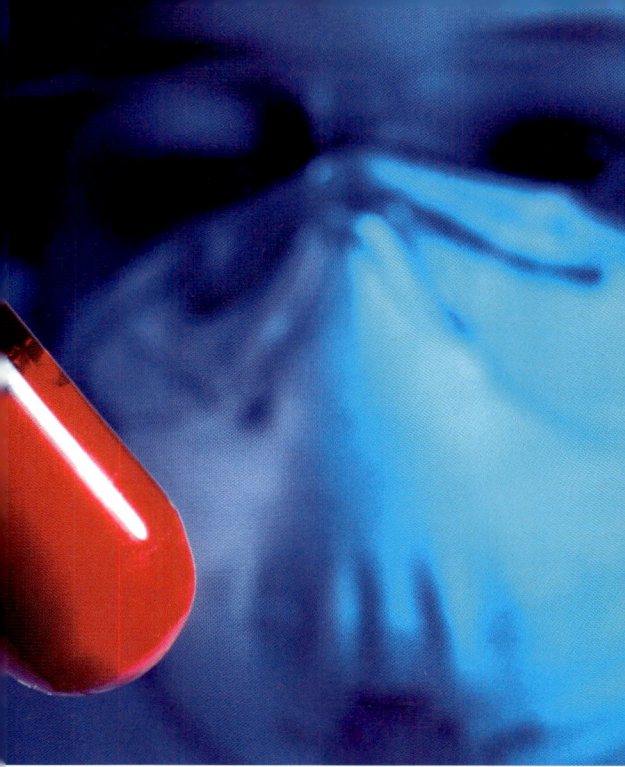

This tube has been spun at high speed to separate the blood cells (red) so that viruses can be isolated in the clear fluid.

(IAVI). A vaccine would have many advantages – people would have more control over their prevention efforts and it would be cheaper than using drugs to treat HIV, as there would be no need for monitoring. Also, children could be protected.

Microbiocides are another approach to HIV infection. These chemicals kill the virus before they enter the cell. They could be inserted into the vagina or anus before or during intercourse. There are 15 microbiocides being tested on humans now.

INVESTIGATING THE EVIDENCE: AIDS VACCINE TRIAL IN THAILAND

The investigation: The RV 144 is the most encouraging trial of vaccines against HIV/AIDS to date. It is the first one to find that a combination of vaccines can actually reduce the risk of HIV infection in humans.

The scientists: RV 144 was led by US Army researchers. Their partners were the Thai Ministry of Public Health; the US National Institute of Allergy and Infectious Diseases; sanofi pasteur, which makes one vaccine, ALVAC; and Global Solutions for Infectious Diseases, which developed AIDSVAX, the other vaccine.

Collecting the evidence: The trial began recruiting 16,000 adult volunteers aged 18–30 in 2003 from Chon Buri and Rayong, two provinces of Thailand where HIV infection rates are high. They were given either ALVAC and then AIDSVAX as a booster, or a placebo (inactive) vaccination.

The conclusion: The vaccine reduced the risk of HIV infection by 31 per cent – 74 in the placebo group became infected compared to 51 in the vaccination group. Larger trials need to be carried out.

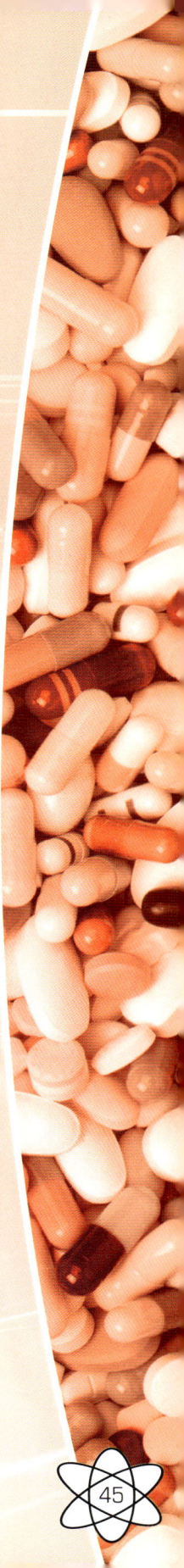

CHAPTER SEVEN

DIAGNOSIS AND TREATMENT

THE MORE RESEARCHERS LEARN ABOUT A NEW DISEASE, THE SOONER THEY CAN OFFER PATIENTS TESTS TO DIAGNOSE IT AND TREATMENTS THAT CAN PREVENT, CONTROL OR CURE IT. HIV/AIDS IS NO EXCEPTION. SOON AFTER THE VIRUS WAS DISCOVERED, IN 1985, THE FIRST HIV TEST WAS DEVELOPED. TWO YEARS LATER, THE FIRST ANTI-VIRAL DRUG, AZT, WAS AVAILABLE.

HOPE AND SURVIVAL

The first HIV test, still used today, depended on finding antibodies to HIV. At first, the HIV antibody test was only used to screen the blood supply – an urgent need because people were becoming infected with HIV from contaminated blood donations. Two years later, the test was used for people to find out if they were HIV-positive.

No one really knew if treatment would work, so AIDS was seen very much as a death sentence. Not surprisingly, many people did not want to know that they were HIV-positive. After the appearance of AZT, the fear of an HIV-positive diagnosis began to decrease, and today, increasing numbers of HIV-positive people survive. This brings different challenges. People with HIV/AIDS have their treatment monitored with ongoing tests of T-cell counts and viral loads. They are also treated with other drugs in case they develop any infections or other AIDS-related problems. However, the drugs that control HIV and mean that many of those infected do not develop AIDS, are not a cure for the disease. A vaccine is still the best hope.

These are crystals of AZT (azidothymidine), the anti-viral drug used by many people to block the development of the HIV virus.

In this ELISA test for antibodies to the HIV virus, a colour change has taken place in six of the wells containing human serum, which means a positive test for the AIDS virus.

HIV TESTING

There are various reasons why HIV testing is done. It is needed to protect the blood supply and to find out the level of infection. Individuals can be tested if they have symptoms, if they are pregnant or if they want to know their HIV status. HIV testing plays an important part in preventing the spread of HIV/AIDS and helping those who are infected.

ELISA

Most HIV tests detect the antibody to the virus. For example, the test called enzyme-linked immunosorbent assay (ELISA) produces a colour response when HIV-antibody binds to a chemical. But people do not usually produce antibodies until three to six months after they have been infected. During the so-called 'window' between infection and antibody production, they will test negative but still be infectious. If they test positive, it is confirmed by a second test called a Western Blot, which uses a different technique.

The antibody test is done on a blood sample – taken from the arm with a needle or from a fingerprick – or on a sample of saliva. People used to have to wait for days or weeks to get the results of an HIV test but now it can be done on the same day. There are also tests that will detect the virus in blood. One, introduced in 1996, tests for a protein called p24 which is found in the HIV virus and appears in the blood just a couple of weeks after infection. Another, called the nucleic acid test, relies on a technique called the polymerase chain reaction (PCR). This multiplies the number of molecules of the virus' genetic materials, rather like photocopying increases the number of sheets of printed material.

This OraQuick antibody test is designed to detect HIV-1 or HIV-2 in saliva, blood or plasma within 20 minutes. The test is used as an aid in the diagnosis of HIV infection.

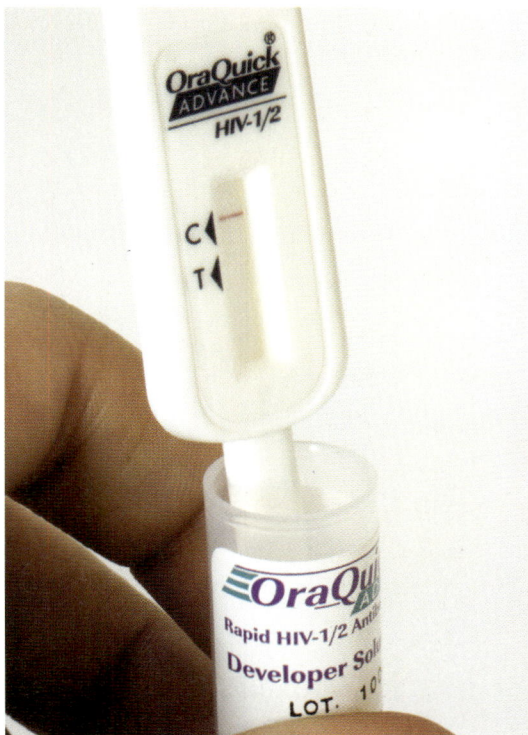

A CAREER AS A HEALTH ADVISER

Gill Carter trained as a social worker and has been a health adviser for 13 years. She works at a sexual health clinic in London in the UK.

A DAY IN THE LIFE OF …

Part of Gill's job is to offer people counselling both before and after they have an HIV test, which may be done as part of a general sexual health screen. She sees people of all ages and backgrounds. In her job, she needs to be patient, calm and never forget that she is there to support the patient in his or her choice to have a test. She also needs to let them choose who to share the result with and never make the decision for them. If the HIV test is negative, Gill will take the opportunity to remind the patient about prevention through safer sex. If the test is positive, she has to be prepared for the patient to be unreasonably angry with her for telling them, and make sure that she does not take this anger personally.

THE HEALTH ADVISER SAYS …

"Some of the people I see are being listened to for the very first time. It is the first time they have been able to share their worries. The best thing about this work is that it is an opportunity to make a difference. You could even save a life."

NEW TREATMENT

There is now drug treatment for HIV that can slow down the rate at which the virus **replicates** itself. The drugs are **ARVs** (anti-retrovirals) and they attack HIV in different ways. A combination of drugs works better than a single drug.

ARVs

There are four main kinds of ARVs. They all allow the infected person to live with HIV because they stop the formation of new HIV particles. The first three work by blocking enzymes that the virus needs to reproduce itself. Enzymes speed up chemical reactions that are necessary to living things – without the enzymes of the digestive system it would take several months to complete a meal. Reverse transcriptase (RT) is one of the main enzymes that HIV needs to reproduce its genetic material. The first two classes of ARVs work by blocking RT. One is called 'nukes' (nucleoside/nucleotide RT inhibitors) and the other 'non'nukes' (non-nucleoside RT inhibitors). Finally, the latest kind of ARV is called a fusion inhibitor and it stops HIV from entering the cell by stopping the virus from sticking onto its surface.

COMBINATIONS

But ARVs are not 100 per cent effective. Some virus particles escape their attack and as they multiply, they change slightly,

---

The scan on the left shows the brain of a normal subject and the scan in the centre an AIDS patient suffering from dementia. The scan on the right shows the same patient after 13 weeks of AZT drug treatment.

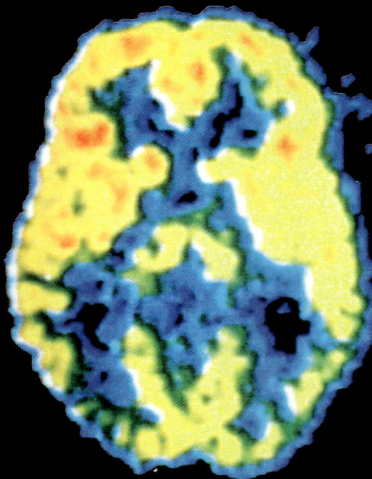

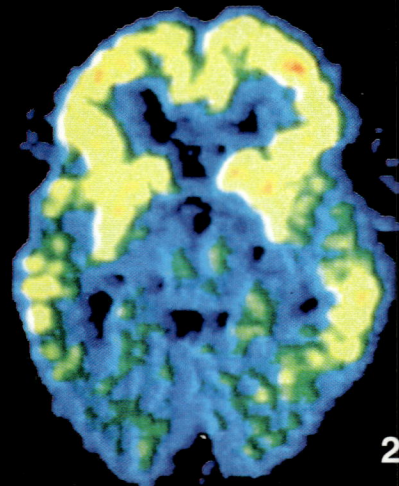

1

2

because their genetic material is never copied perfectly. These new strains, as they are called, may be resistant to ARVs which were designed to attack the original strain. Patients are usually treated with a combination of drugs – if the strain of HIV is resistant to one drug, it may not be to a second, third or fourth. The combination of three or more ARVs is usually known as Highly Active Antiretroviral Therapy (HAART). There are more than 20 ARVs that can be prescribed and many different combinations.

Taking HAART requires total commitment. The person with HIV will have to take tablets for the rest of his or her life. Some ARVs have side-effects, such as tiredness and feeling sick. The person with HIV may start taking ARVs before they actually feel ill. However, ARVs do offer people who are HIV-positive the chance of many years of a life free of AIDS.

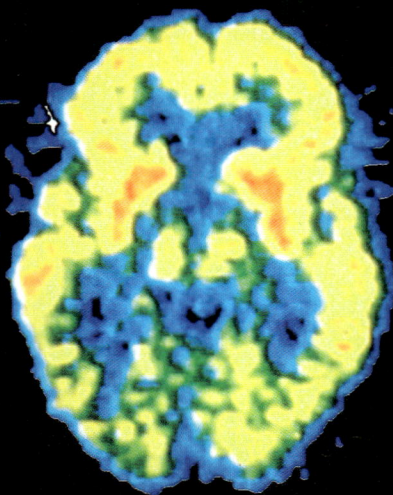

INVESTIGATING THE EVIDENCE: TRIAL OF A COMBINATION THERAPY

The investigation: HAART is complicated, because more than one drug is involved. But scientists needed to know which drugs are best included in the drug 'cocktail'.

The scientists: Yazdan Yazdanpanah, researcher at the University Service for Infectious Disease and Travel Medicine in Tourcoing, France, working with colleagues in the UK and Switzerland.

Collecting the evidence: The researchers wanted to compare drug combinations based on a protease inhibitor (PI) with those based on non-nucleoside reverse transcriptase inhibitors ('non-nukes'). The team took an indirect approach and 'mined' existing information. They found 14 clinical trials of 6,785 patients with AIDS on a number of combinations of drugs involving PIs and non-nukes. They looked at the survival rates of the patients.

The conclusion: Triple therapy gave a better survival rate than dual therapy. And there was a better survival rate for drug combinations based on a PI than those based on non-nukes. The researchers would now like to see trials that compare the combinations.

AROUND THE WORLD

Most sufferers live in countries that would not normally be able to afford ARVs. But there are ways in which the drugs can be made available. The drug companies can give them out free, or once a new drug has been discovered, chemists can **synthesize** the molecule and make cheap, **generic** copies. The only thing preventing them is a **patent** – the legal control that inventors assert over their discoveries.

So, if an HIV drug was discovered in 1984, then no one could have sold a version until 2004 – the year that the patent came to an end. The generic version can be made in countries where there is no patent protection and where manufacturing costs are low. Currently, generic versions of ARVs are being made in places such as India and Latin America. WHO (the World Health Organization) says there are about 6.5 million people around the world who urgently need ARVs, but only 15 per cent are getting the drugs.

REACHING PATIENTS

In Brazil, in South America, people with HIV/AIDS have had access to the drugs for many years. And Botswana and Uganda

in Africa are expanding their ARV programmes. However, in sub-Saharan Africa as a whole, treatment coverage is only 11 per cent (that is, nearly five million need the drugs and only half a million are currently getting them).

REACHING THE SICK

When people become sick with AIDS, they need antibiotics for life-threatening infections and their families need practical help and emotional support. For all this, a country needs a network of clinics and hospitals, staffed by well-qualified nurses, doctors and health workers. In countries that are 'resource poor', especially when they are affected by war and political problems, this is a huge challenge.

Public awareness is an important factor in the treatment of HIV/AIDS. Here, schoolchildren in Ethiopia celebrate a national AIDS day.

INVESTIGATING THE EVIDENCE: CAN ANYONE WHO NEEDS TO, BE TREATED?

The investigation: Most countries affected by HIV/AIDS try to get treatment to at least 80 per cent of those who need it. Big international projects are needed to provide the drive and resources to improve access to HIV diagnostics, drugs and monitoring services. The latest is the 'All by 2010' project.

The leaders: The 'All by 2010' project is led by the G8 nations (the group of the world's richest countries) with other countries' leaders at the UN Summit.

The project: People with HIV have to be made aware of the life-long nature of treatment with antiretroviral drugs. For this, they need ongoing monitoring and support, which means building up a country's healthcare infrastructure. The drugs must be made available at low cost, which means bringing pharmaceutical companies on board as partners. Facilities for testing and counselling have to be developed alongside the treatment facilities. The 'All by 2010' plan is part of the UN's Millennium Development Goal 6 which pledges to halt and begin to reverse the upward trend of HIV/AIDS by 2015.

The conclusion: In 2008, the heads of UNAIDS, UNICEF and WHO admitted that most countries would not meet the 2010 target. Some progress has

CHAPTER EIGHT

AIDS AND THE FUTURE

HIV/AIDS IS ON THE INCREASE ALMOST EVERYWHERE, BUT THE SITUATION IS GETTING WORSE IN SOME COUNTRIES AND IMPROVING IN OTHERS. IN KENYA, ZIMBABWE AND BURKINA FASO, SOME GROUPS OF THE POPULATION ARE BEGINNING TO SHOW A DECREASE IN THE NUMBER OF CASES OF HIV/AIDS. HOWEVER, IN EASTERN EUROPE AND CENTRAL ASIA, THERE HAVE BEEN BIG INCREASES.

TAKING ACTION

In 2001, the United Nations declared HIV/AIDS a global emergency and said that massive action is required to defeat it. One of the UN's eight Millennium Development Goals for the world is to halve and reverse the spread of HIV/AIDS by the year 2015.

In 1967, the WHO began a campaign of mass vaccination to rid the world of smallpox. Ten years later, a cook in Ethiopia became the last person in the world to contract smallpox. The WHO then decided to eradicate polio, and has made a lot of progress towards it in many countries. Central to eradication are National Immunization Days, when volunteers visit each home and give polio vaccines to any child under five. So why cannot HIV also be eradicated?

First, an effective vaccine is needed. Even then, wiping out HIV may be tricky, because the virus tends to mutate so easily. Scientists are doing all they can to outwit HIV with research, but it is possible that HIV will win. We may never get rid of, or even control it.

A baby in Sierra Leone, west Africa, is vaccinated against HIV/AIDS.

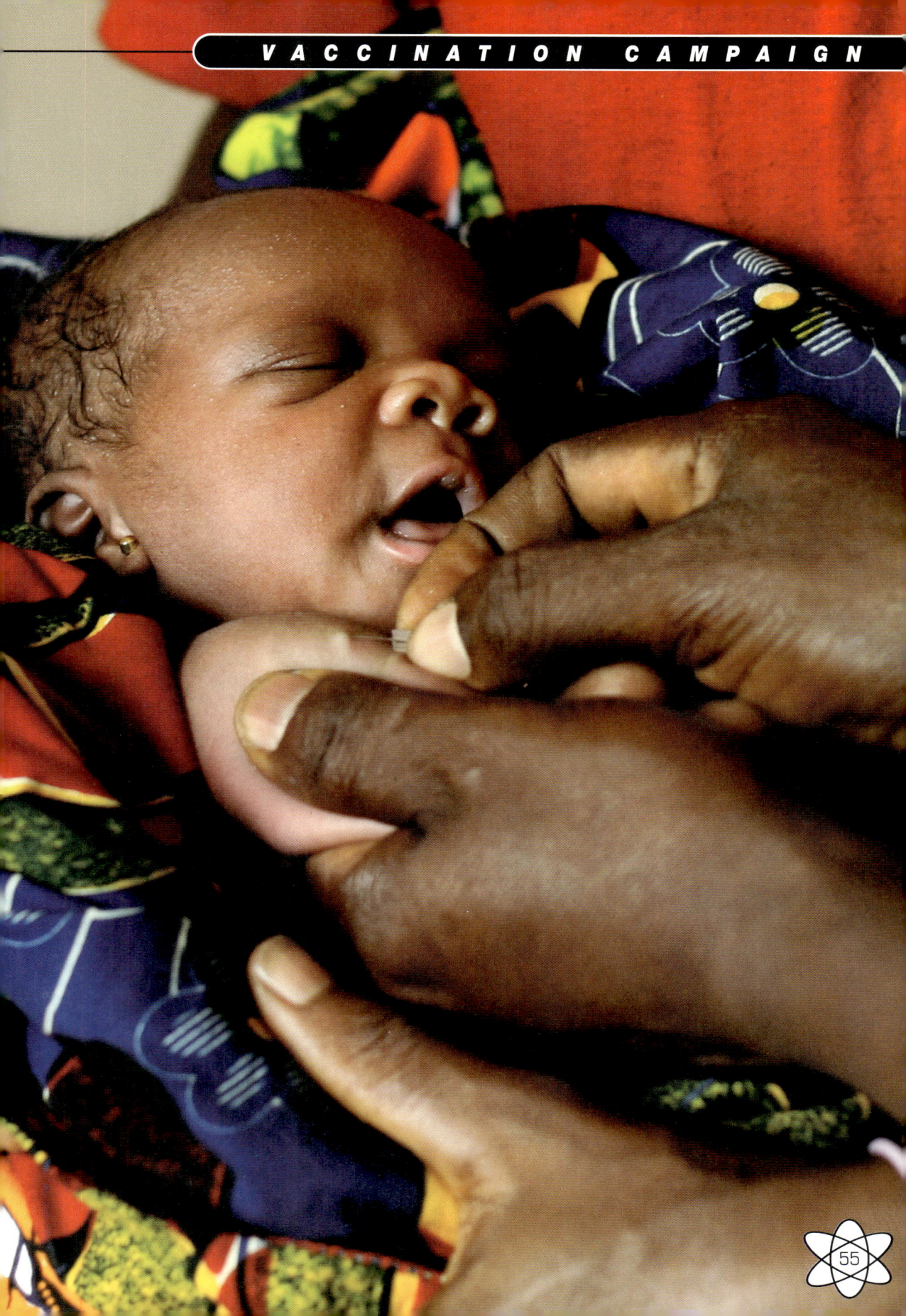

In Hong Kong in 2003, people wore face masks in an attempt to avoid contracting SARS (severe acute respiratory syndrome) that threatened to become pandemic.

EPIDEMICS AND PANDEMICS

An epidemic is a sudden increase in the number of cases of a disease over and above the expected level. A pandemic is an epidemic that affects a large area – a continent or the whole world.

HIV/AIDS is a pandemic disease with serious epidemic outbreaks in various places around the world, including eastern Europe, Asia and sub-Saharan Africa. In many ways, the HIV/AIDS pandemic took the world by surprise. The global response has seemed to be slow because the virus had a headstart on the scientists.

The latest pandemic fears – bird flu and swine flu – are the old enemy dressed in different clothes. Influenza is classified according to the nature of two proteins that 'clothe' the surface of the virus. There are 16 types of a protein called hemagluttinin (H) and 9 of a protein called neuraminidase (N). This leads to many different H and N combinations, known as subtypes, of influenza. Subtypes can be further classified into strains which vary as to how pathogenic (dangerous) they are. H5N1 bird flu can spread to humans through contact with infected birds and there have been many cases reported since 1997. Bird flu can be deadly to humans but the spread from person to person is rare. The question now is whether the H1N1 swine flu virus could undergo genetic changes

▶ ▶ http://kidshealth.levinechildrenshospital.org/PageManager.jsp?dn=levinechildrenshospital&article_set=70004&lic=236&cat_id=20174

Bird flu, contracted through contact with infected birds, can be deadly to humans.

that would make it easy to transmit from person to person, possibly causing a pandemic.

FIGHTING BACK

There are two weapons against such pandemics – vaccination and anti-viral drugs. Scientists have created a vaccine but it will need to be produced on a large scale to stop a pandemic. There are two anti-viral drugs that can treat bird/swine flu known as Tamiflu (oseltamivir) and Relenza (zanamivir). Like the ARVs needed to treat AIDS, there could be problems getting the drugs to everyone who needs them. Pandemics are unpredictable. Everyone must be made aware of the potential dangers and governments must put action plans in place at once.

INVESTIGATING THE EVIDENCE: HAS BIRD FLU REACHED BRITAIN?

The investigation: Surveying wild birds in Britain for bird flu.

The scientists: The bird survey team at the Veterinary Laboratories Agency, the Wildfowl and Wetlands Trust and the British Association for Shooting and Conservation. The scientists are helped by reports from the general public.

Collecting the evidence: Wild birds, including the European white-fronted goose, wigeon, teal and mallard, are caught, tagged with a ring and have samples of their droppings collected for analysis in the laboratory. Samples are also taken from shot birds (from legal wildfowling activity). Finally, members of the public are asked to report to the VLA if they find ten or more dead birds in the same place at the same time (five or more in Scotland) as this may indicate an outbreak of bird flu.

The conclusion: Although the UK was officially declared free of bird flu in November 2008, some small outbreaks of the disease have been noted. There was one in Dorset in January 2009 and outbreaks in Suffolk and Norfolk in the previous year. Prompt action by the VLA and other agencies stopped these outbreaks from spreading.

FUTURE RESEARCH

What are researchers hoping to discover next? Scientists have been studying infection ever since the 19th century, when the 'germ' theory of disease became widely accepted. Research on important infectious diseases has already saved millions of lives, but many people have died because the scientific discoveries were not put into practice soon enough. We have learned a lot about HIV/AIDS in the last 30 years, but there is still much more to be discovered. The main priority is to find a vaccine against HIV that really works.

Modern medicine and biology revolves around understanding the body, the cell and microbes at the level of molecules and genes. This means that the HIV virus can be 'dissected' in the laboratory to understand what the key protein molecules are. Currently, vaccines are being based on these molecular components rather than the whole virus. It would be very dangerous to even try to use the latter because the recipients might become infected as a result. However, the molecules cannot be injected on their own. They need to be carried on a vehicle or vector. Scientists are using various – harmless – viruses as vectors.

This electron micrograph shows what a scientist would see in a laboratory – an infected T-cell with its typical lumpy appearance, and small, spherical virus particles (coloured green) budding away from the cell membrane.

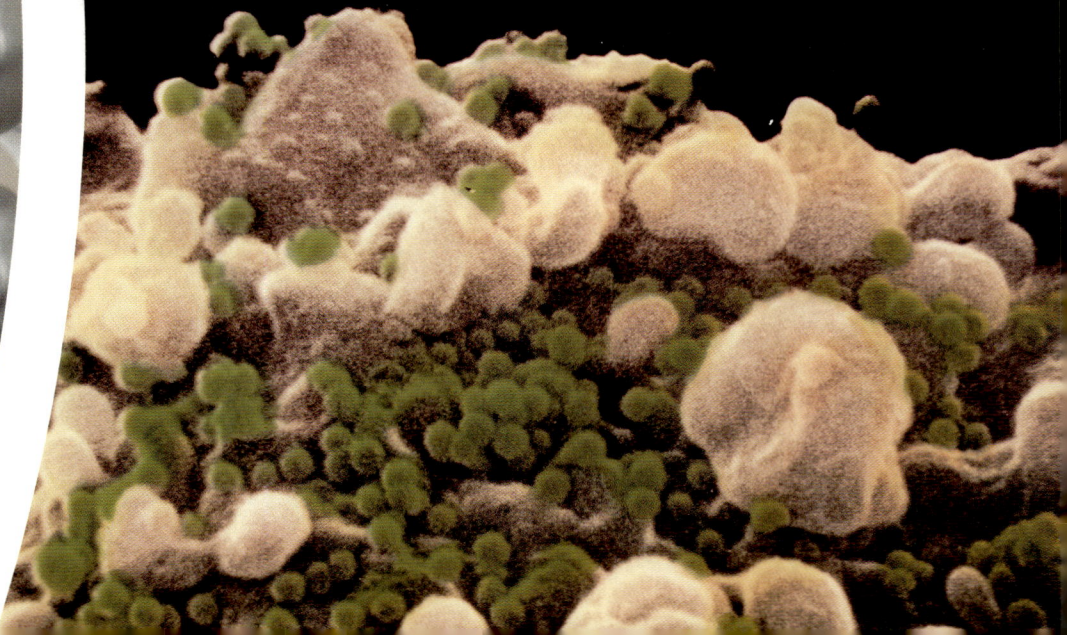

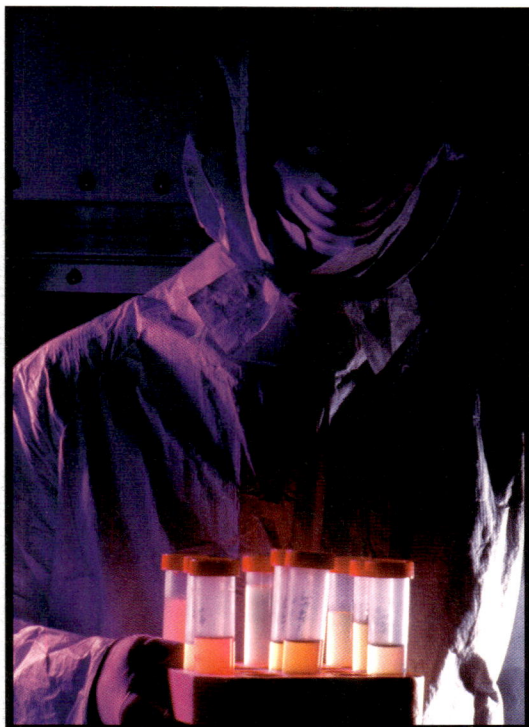

A researcher works on test tubes that contain the HIV virus grown in a culture medium. By better understanding the virus itself, scientists hope to be able to develop drugs and vaccines.

VACCINATION

There are two kinds of HIV vaccine that could be developed. One conventional kind would prevent infection from taking hold. The other would be a therapeutic vaccine that slows the progress of the disease once a person has become infected.

It is always easier to prevent a disease than to treat it. An approach that combines contraception (birth control) with HIV prevention is the microbiocide – a gel that a woman can apply to the vagina. Several types of microbiocide are being developed and tested.

A CAREER IN SCIENCE

Dr Moira Bode is a researcher in the discovery chemistry group at the Council for Scientific and Industrial Research, South Africa. The organization is one of the leading scientific and technology research and development organizations in Africa and is supported by the South African government.

A DAY IN THE LIFE OF …

Moira's project began in 1994 and it aims to reduce the cost of preparing nucleoside reverse transcriptase inhibitors by simplifying the chemical steps used to manufacture them. The breakthrough for the project has been to use enzymes, rather than chemical catalysts, in one stage of the process. The enzymes come from microbes and Moira's team have been screening different strains to get the best enzymes. The laboratory work therefore combines both chemistry and microbiology. The project will help more South Africans with HIV/AIDS to gain access to anti-retroviral drugs.

THE SCIENTIST SAYS …

"Much development work was undertaken to make this into a viable process. The belief the team had in the process and its potential was largely responsible for their determination to make it work."

LOOKING TO THE FUTURE

HIV/AIDS is the first pandemic that has happened in the era of modern medical research. Scientists have been able to use sophisticated technology to investigate the disease. They have identified HIV – which was previously unknown – and sensitive tests for infection that can be used the world over. An understanding of the life cycle of the virus has been the basis of developing the ARVs, which can interrupt and slow down the disease. Research is definitely saving lives, but many more people could benefit if the knowledge that has been gained is applied where it is needed.

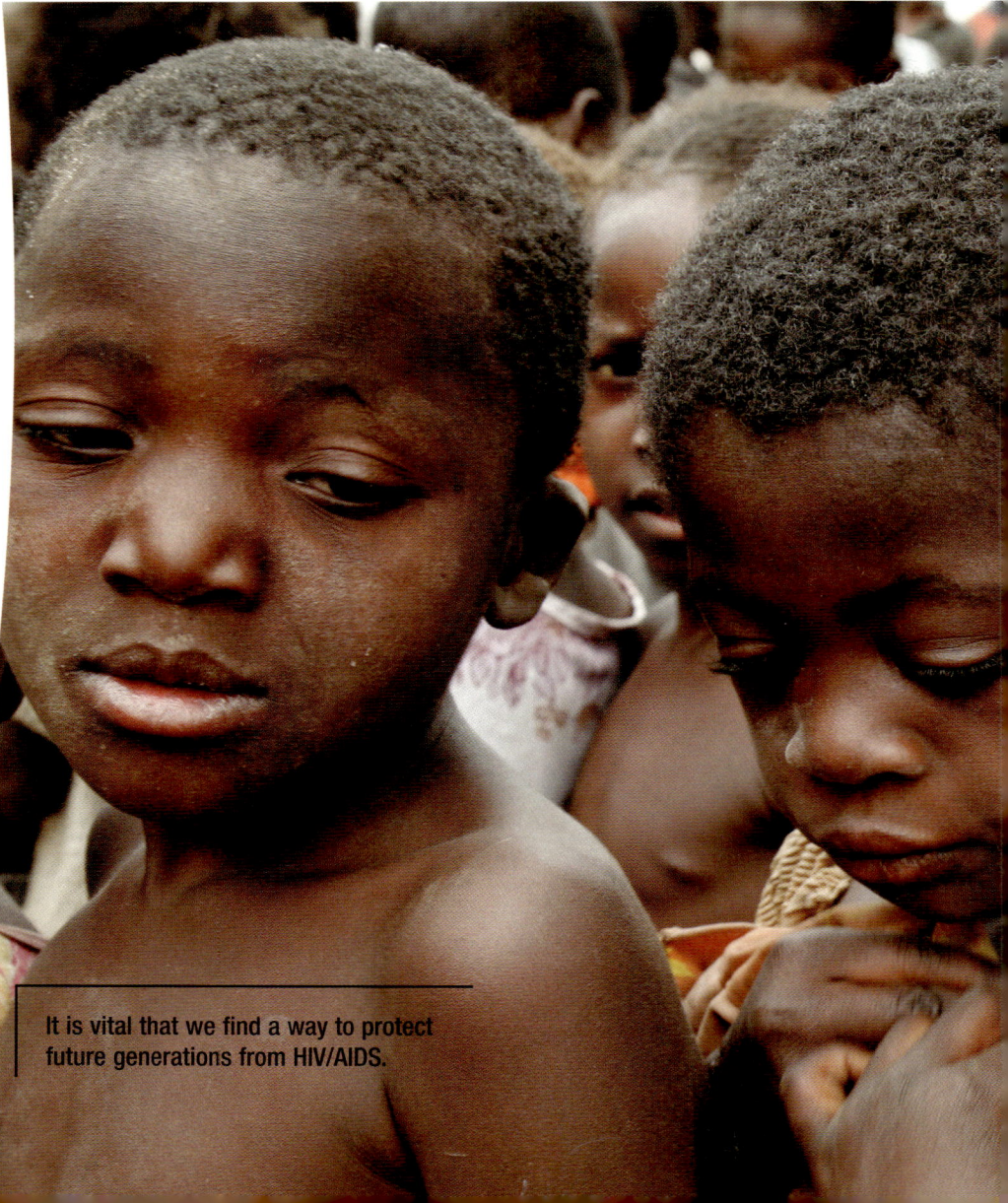

It is vital that we find a way to protect future generations from HIV/AIDS.

There have been some significant achievements in HIV/AIDS research but the real challenge is bringing research discoveries to all of those affected by HIV/AIDS. This is the responsibility of many people – governments, organizations such as the WHO, and local clinics and community projects. There is still so much to be done to educate people in the risks of contracting HIV through unsafe sex and injecting drugs, as well as ensuring the safety of the blood supply and medical injections. Research will bring more benefits, such as better drugs and an effective vaccine. But they must be made available because the global toll of AIDS still continues to increase.

anaemia a condition where there is less of the oxygen-carrying protein haemoglobin in the blood, often occurring because of iron deficiency

antibiotics drugs that either kill or slow the growth of bacteria and are used to cure bacterial (but not viral) infections

antibody a protein produced by the immune system in response to infection

ARVs anti-retroviral drugs; these are a type of treatment for AIDS that blocks part of the HIV natural life cycle

blood transfusion the replacement of lost blood by blood or blood products, usually donated by another

CDC the United States Center for Disease Control and Prevention, that leads the fight against infectious diseases including HIV/AIDS

cell the smallest unit of a living organism; there are around 200 different types of cell in the human body

clot a plug formed from blood cells that stops blood escaping from the body after injury

contagious diseases spread by touch or direct contact with a contaminated object are said to be contagious

dementia a brain disease where there is loss of memory and other mental capabilities

disease an abnormal condition of the body, arising from many different causes, including infection

DNA deoxyribonucleic acid, the chemical from which our genetic blueprint is made

enzyme a biological catalyst that speeds up chemical reactions occurring in the human body and in other living things

epidemic a serious outbreak of many cases of a disease over a short period of time

generic describes a copy of a drug where the exclusive patent lifetime has run out

genetic affected or affecting genes, the segments of DNA that control heredity

haemophilia a blood disorder where the lack of a protein called Factor VIII means that the blood does not clot properly

host an organism that provides nourishment for a parasite

immune being protected against a disease because the immune system has mounted a defence

lymph gland or lymph nodes, are found in the lymphatic system, where they help fight infection

microbe short for microorganism; organisms that can only be seen under a microscope and include bacteria, fungi, viruses and protozoa

microbiocides substances that kill microbes

molecule a group of two or more atoms that make up a substance

mucous membrane the lining of most of the body's cavities, such as the mouth and the intestines

mutated describes a change in the DNA sequence of the genome that, in viruses, may help it to evade treatment that previously worked

nucleus a structure within a cell that contains its DNA

pandemic a worldwide epidemic

parasite an organism that lives off another organism

patent the rights over an invention, such as a drug, that means that for a period of time it cannot be copied

placebo an inactive treatment given for comparison purposes in a clinical trial in a laboratory

protein a large, complex molecule found in living things

receptor a protein molecule on a cell's surface that can cause some kind of reaction

replicates copies DNA when a cell divides so that a fresh copy goes into each new cell

retrovirus a virus, such as HIV, where the genome consists of RNA, not DNA

RNA ribonucleic acid; similar in chemical nature to DNA, but with different roles in the cell

SARS severe acute respiratory syndrome; a highly contagious type of pneumonia

synthesize to make a chemical compound through a series of chemical reactions

vaccination giving a substance (vaccine) to someone to stimulate their immune system to protect against a disease

virus the smallest of the microbes; it requires a host in order to survive

WHO World Health Organization, an agency of the United Nations